HEALING DREAMS

RUSS PARKER

Healing Dreams

THEIR POWER AND PURPOSE IN YOUR SPIRITUAL LIFE

Foreword by Anne Long

Crossroad • New York

1989
The Crossroad Publishing Company
370 Lexington Avenue, New York, N.Y. 10017

Printed in the United States of America

Library of Congress Cataloging-in-Publication Data

Parker, Russ.
   Healing dreams : their power and purpose in your spiritual life /
Russ Parker : foreword by Anne Long.
      p.   cm.
   Bibliography: p.
   ISBN 0-8245-0922-6
   1. Dreams—Religious aspects—Christianity.   2. Spiritual healing.
I. Title.
BF1099.S76P37   1989
154.6'3—dc19   88-30370
                                                               CIP

Contents

Acknowledgements

I would like to take this opportunity to thank all those friends who have encouraged me in the writing of this book. They include Dr Brian Taylor who helped me to believe that I have something to say. My thanks also to members of the Grove Spirituality Group who encouraged me to begin writing on the subject of dreams; they include Graham Piggott, Ann Long, Ian Bunting, Richard Baukam, Roger Pooley, Ian Williams and Michael Vasey – to name but a few. I am especially grateful to all those who have trusted me with their dreams and given me the privilege of working with them for healing in the name of Jesus.

I would also like to thank Yvonne, my secretary, for patiently wading through my material and typing it out.

Last, but by no means least, my thanks to Carole, my wife, for her support and encouragement, and to our children, Emma and Joel, I give my love and thanks for being so understanding, for when Dad was not at play it was because he had to work.

Foreword

Here is a readable book which throws light on what it is for many of us a mysterious and sometimes disturbing part of our lives.

I first met the author, Russ Parker, when he was a student at St John's College, Nottingham, training for ordination into the Church of England ministry. I was his tutor and soon came to appreciate this quiet, friendly, relaxed Merseysider. When I discovered he was embarking on a postgraduate thesis on dreams I was more than a little curious. Yet I soon got to know Russ as an industrious person concerned for biblical and theological integrity while at the same time drawn towards psychology and counselling.

One day in the tutorial group Russ asked if any of us had any interesting dreams he could include in his project. After the predictable guffaws it suddenly occurred to me that when I was under pressure my sleep was so disturbed by a recurring nightmare which I could well do without. Nothing daunted, Russ took me on. With sensitivity and prayer he helped me to examine the meaning and purpose of my dream. Fresh light was given, new insights gained, and a burden was lifted – the nightmares stopped.

This book shows how God uses dreams to give guidance and healing. I hope it will help others as I have been helped, both in their own lives and in the pastoral care they offer others in their Christian ministry.

REV. ANNE LONG

Pastoral Consultant

Acorn Christian Healing Trust

1 I Have a Dream

For the last ten years or so I have been working with other people's dreams. It has been an exciting journey into the realms of spiritual growth and healing through the power of Jesus Christ. Yet I had to be converted to the usefulness of dreams for personal growth and spiritual renewal. As a Christian minister from a conservative Evangelical background, I had inherited a scepticism for anything mystical or which smacked of coming from the psychic fringe. I thought nothing much of dreams and imagined that they were the random wanderings of the sleeping mind or the result of too much rich food the night before. Taking dreams seriously did not fit into my understanding of proper Christian behaviour and anyone who thought otherwise was immediately suspect, according to my theological outlook.

I have since come to realize that my theological horizon was not wide enough to take in what was plainly illustrated within the Bible. I discovered an amazing amount of material on dreams and also visions, a companion experience. I had never allowed myself to truly respond to such a weight of biblical material before. I began to be convinced that, as a Christian, I must take such evidence far more seriously.

This book has been written to provide both a biblical and practical guide to the whole experience of dreaming. I shall also outline some of the basic discoveries made about the actual process of sleep and dreaming, and shall describe some of the major beliefs about dreams held by the pioneers of dream interpretation such as Freud and Jung. However, we shall need to hold to our Christian foundations in the Bible, so I shall provide some biblical insights about dreams to show how God can and does use dreams to bring about guidance and healing for his people. Since working with dreams I have been increasingly grateful to God for showing me how, by his grace, he can use us to reach into many of our unresolved problems and hurts. They are all too often caught in our dreams and, by taking these seriously and with respect, we are able to bring Christ's healing and relief to the buried hurts reflected in our dreams. Therefore I have written this book to encourage you to use your own dreams, as well as those of the people we seek to help, as one more

resource among others to bring about the wholeness we long to see
in all of us.

There is no shortage of examples of how dreams have helped
people. Besides the evidence of the Bible itself and other ancient
literature, there are the records of such worthies as Kekule and
Einstein who testify to a kind of 'breakthrough' in their discoveries
as a result of their dreams. Innumerable people have shared how a
dream has alerted them to something they had not consciously
noticed before. One example is that of Mrs Frances Vernier who
prevented a fire at a home for the elderly which she managed. She
had dreamt of the building being ablaze and had got out of bed and
driven over to the house, where she searched vigorously until she
discovered a gas pipe aflame.[1]

Clearly, dreams do relate in some measure to our waking lives,
and paying attention to them can offer real benefits. Most of the
counsellors who employ dreams will say how their patients have
taken steps towards recovery when they 'worked' with their own
dreams. So then, what will the Christian Church do with dreams?
To relegate them to the area of fringe interest cuts right against the
grain of the Bible and ignores the benefits that secular society has
gained from a proper response to dreams. It is my belief that God
gives us dreams as a benefit inseparable from the gift of sleep to
which the psalmist refers (Ps. 127.2). As Christians we need to
recover a proper respect and use of dreams and visions, so that we
do not miss out on the good gifts which our heavenly Father has
given to his children.

My own interest and growth in understanding of dreams was
brought about by a dream which dramatically changed my life.

One morning in 1975, when I was a lay Baptist minister, I was sitting in
my upstairs study preparing notes for a sermon. My eyes were open and
I was awake, but from time to time my mind would drift into a sort of
waking-dream or daydream. The picture that began to form in my mind
was that of an old toy fort which resembled one which I had been given
when I was five years old. Now the fort was of life-sized dimensions and
I was standing right in the middle of it. For some reason I knew that I
was a very young child, and as I looked up at the battlements I could see
Arthurian knights patrolling. I could feel the hot sun on my head and I
felt so safe and warm. Suddenly all this peace and security was shattered.
Out from a square hole in the floor of this old fort came what looked like
a long tongue of huge, sticky fly-paper; it seemed alive and immediately
it grabbed hold of my head. I struggled hard to get free and stay in the
fort but it was a losing battle. Relentlessly I was pulled down through the
hole and driven along a dark tunnel; all the while my face was being
smashed into the walls at either side.

As I sat there in my study that morning I was acutely aware of feelings of rage and anger rising up from deep within me.

What was really startling about this dream was that, as the feelings of anger began to come to the surface, there came a string of memories all of which contained the same expression of angry rage. The most immediate was from a few days earlier. It had been my turn to baby-sit with our son Joel, and I had been at it from about midnight until the early hours of the following day before he drifted off into sleep. However, an hour or so later he woke up and started crying again; my wife was fast asleep in another room, and after all it was still my shift. I can remember feeling really angry at him being awake, only this time when I lifted him out of his cot it was not to give him comfort but to take out on him my anger. I completely lost control and began to shout at him and strangle him. It was only the intervention of my wife which prevented any physical damage from being done. I felt so ashamed of myself; here I was, a Christian minister strangling the life out of my son like an angry vandal.

I had had a number of these outbursts in my life and I had prayed about them, but nothing seemed changed in my behaviour. I wanted to be free but felt really trapped in my feelings. It is interesting to note, by the way, that the dream was triggered by a recent experience and that this is often the reason why we have certain dreams.

The rest of the memories were all directly connected with my mother. When I was about ten years old my mum asked me to run down to Parson's corner shop to buy some cigarettes for her. I was enjoying a game of football in the street with all my friends and my two brothers and sisters. I felt picked on and, I remembered, I ran off to do the errand in sheer rage at this and called my mother all the swear words I could think of as I went.

The other memory was of a later time, when one of the boys from our street was told to move away from our house; apparently he was sitting on our fence and my Mum told him to go up to his own house and play. Sydney was his name and he climbed back on that fence just as soon as my Mum had disappeared into the house and he began to call out loudly, 'Mrs Parker is a dirty old cow.' My Mum was having none of this and so she sent out my younger brother to hit him and send him packing. The job was duly done, but Sydney was not to be dismissed that easily. I was in the house that day and I knew in my heart that my Mum would ask me to go out next and I just hated the thought of it. Well, the command for me to go and do likewise came. I went out and I could feel the cold anger beginning to well up inside of me against my mother, and when I reached Sydney I put my hands around his throat and began to squeeze hard. He began to choke and I had to be dragged off him. The anger was directed at my Mum but Sydney had become the focus for it. I suddenly grew afraid at how I felt towards my Mum but there was no reason I could think of for feeling like this.

These and other memories linked up to the dream picture, and I could feel them all with the same intensity as if they were actually happening again. I have already mentioned the times I had prayed for help over my feelings, but now it seemed that I was beginning to get somewhere. I believe that this waking dream was a gift from God and that he gave me the presence of mind to write it down straightaway before I forgot it. And so I hurried downstairs to share it with my wife Carole who was working in the kitchen. I made her stop everything and sit down to listen.

Her immediate reply was to say that the dream seemed to be a symbol of being born (having been both a nurse and a mum probably helped to give her this immediate insight). The sticky fly-paper was the umbilical cord and the dark tunnel was the birth passage. Instinctively I felt this was right, and as I began to acknowledge that my feelings of anger could in fact be related to how I was born, I knew that I was on the trail toward being healed. But couldn't all this be just a bit too far-fetched? After all, what is in a dream? I began to be a little concerned that I might be running away with myself and getting out of my depth. And on top of all this, there were the real difficulties in our relationships with my mother that stood in the way.

She had had a very hard life and had been divorced from my father for about seven years by this time. Her health had suffered and in her own eyes she had lost everything that had meant so much to her; her home had gone and the man she still loved was married now to someone else. Consequently she had retreated into a world of make-believe. Her switched-on television was her constant companion; she seldom went out or visited anyone. She would tell me stories of having been approached by handsome men on the bus who asked her for a date. We all knew that she was fantasizing and compensating for the break-up of her marriage. Needless to say, I felt more than reluctant to go to see my mother and ask her, 'How was I born?' But go I did.

I asked her if she could remember anything or was she drugged up at the time. Very calmly she told me that I had been born at home and that she was fully aware of the events. 'Your birth was as normal as all the rest,' she said, 'except for one thing. You were born with an enlarged head and they had difficulty in getting your head to come out, or so the doctor said, and you didn't need a slap to make you take your first breath. You came out kicking and shouting and with the most brilliant red hair I had ever seen on a baby. You looked like a carrot.' Apparently I got the nick-name Rusty which, with the passage of time, became Russell.

I can remember being profoundly moved as I listened to my mother and I felt very tearful. Some hurt deep inside me was being touched and I welcomed it. I also felt a new regard for my mother and so, very deliberately, I asked for her forgiveness for all the anger and hate I had felt in the years gone by. 'It's a bit late in the day I know,' I said, 'but I mean it, Mum, please forgive me.' I wasn't really prepared for what happened next. My mother told me that I was the first person in her whole life who had asked forgiveness of her. She then told me all about her life and childhood. Her mother had died when she was three, and so she was raised by her half-sister who had an affair with her father. She had been beaten as a child and had felt lonely all her life. She married my father during the early years of the war and there had been many difficulties which resulted in an affair and the birth of a daughter. Apparently my father came home on compassionate leave and gave my mother the choice of saving the marriage by giving up her daughter or keeping her daughter but ending the marriage and losing her son. She gave away her baby girl, but had felt guilty all these years and, thirty-five years later, still longed to see her daughter again. 'Can God ever forgive me?' she asked. I told her that if God could forgive me my sins he could surely forgive hers too. So she asked me to pray with her and I had the joy of leading my mother to a true faith in Jesus and the knowledge that she had been forgiven. I found this to be one of the most meaningful encounters of my life.

The most notable results of this experience have been the inner healing of my emotions. I have the usual ups and downs like anybody else, but no longer do I have the rage and anger. Jesus has healed me. I became aware of feeling more whole and together than ever before. Secondly, my mother started living in the real world and we found that we could relate normally for the first time as adults. She found a new freedom with the rest of her children, and so was able to share with them her secret and, perhaps for the first time in her life, feel really accepted by those she loved. And thirdly, I began to respect and take notice of my dreams. All this healing and restoration had come about as a result of following through a dream. I believe that this was under the guidance of God. I started to share my experience with others and so began a journey that would teach me the value of dreams for use in healing and deliverance ministry. But I needed a proper foundation and framework to work with dreams, and I found my starting point in the Bible. Here there were further discoveries that would deepen my respect for dreams.

2 The Bible and Dreams

Immediately you open the pages of the Bible and look for the subject of dreams there is a startling contrast with today's popular scepticism of their usefulness. Dreams are respected; they are listened to and generally there is a response to their message. Far from being a topic of fringe interest, they are dealt with in some detail and taken very seriously. There are in the Bible over 130 references to dreams and almost 100 to visions, the bulk of them in the Old Testament. However, we must not underestimate their value in the emerging Church, as both the beginning of the gospel story and the strategy of growth and evangelism are to some degree dependent upon responding to dreams and visions. Herman Riffel goes so far as to say that if we added together all the direct references to dreams and visions, all the stories surrounding them and all the prophecies that issued out of them, we would find that about one-third of the entire Bible is related to our subject.[1] So we can easily conclude that the subject of dreams plays an important role in the whole biblical narrative.

The Bible is very similar in this respect to other ancient Near Eastern writings. Dream libraries, for example, existed at ancient Nineveh as long ago as 5000 BC. In Egypt, Serapis was the god of dreams and he communicated to his devotees as they slept in special temples (*serapiums*). The temple at Memphis was built as long ago as 3000 BC. In fact the oldest surviving work on the interpretation of dreams comes from Egypt, and it lists dreams in various categories depending upon whether they had a good or bad effect upon the sleeper.

Now it needs to be said at this point that amongst many other things that Christians believe, a fundamental article of faith is that we have a God who communicates to those he loves and has created in his image. Both the Old and the New Testaments illustrate the range of ways in which God touches our lives with his words: through the prophetic and written word, by the wonder of nature, by his mighty acts of deliverance and also by dreams. What is so attractive about the latter is the fact that we all dream! It is not the prerogative of the charismatic leader or prophet or mighty man of

faith. Yes, there are those prophets such as Daniel and Jeremiah, and
Ezekiel in particular, who were noted for their dreams and visions;
but there are also the dreams of a sentry on duty (Judg. 7.13–15), the
spoiled teenager (Gen. 37.5) and the worried wife of Pilate (Matt.
27.19). So one basic conclusion we can draw from a preliminary
glance at the Bible is that dreams are a normal experience and,
like any other normal experience, can become a vehicle by which
God can communicate with us. There is no attempt to distinguish
between the experience of ordinary dreaming and dreams through
which God has spoken his message. Therefore they offer a potential
resource for our spiritual growth.

Dreams and Visions

Interestingly enough, the Hebrew term for dream is *harlam* and
comes from a word meaning 'to make whole or healthy'. So right
away there is a clue here to one of the functions of dreaming; it is to
add to our growth in wholeness and completeness as individuals.
No wonder the Psalmist says, 'He grants sleep to those he loves'
(Ps. 127.2). Dreams are a gift from a loving God and they are
intended for our good.

Vision, on the other hand, implies the ability to perceive with an
inner eye. It is a word closely related to the term 'seer', which was
applied to a forerunner of the classical prophet. There is the notion
that those who have visions are in an ecstatic state at the
time. Compare the definition given by Thayer in his Greek–English
Lexicon:

> A sudden emotion whereby one is transported as it were out of himself,
> so that in this rapt condition, although awake, his mind is so drawn off
> from all surrounding objects and wholly fixed on things divine that he
> sees nothing but the forms and images lying within, and thinks that he
> perceives with his bodily eyes and ears realities shown him by God.

Now whilst any spiritual experience is going to involve emotions, it
doesn't follow that the individual has lost his sense of reason and
objectivity. Consider Peter's experience on the rooftop in Joppa:

> About noon the following day ... Peter went up on the roof to pray. He
> became hungry and wanted something to eat, and while the meal was
> being prepared he fell into a trance. He saw heaven opened and some-
> thing like a large sheet being let down to earth by its four corners. It
> contained all kinds of four-footed animals, as well as reptiles of the earth
> and birds of the air. Then a voice told him, 'Get up, Peter, kill and eat.'

'Surely not, Lord!' Peter replied, 'I have never eaten anything unclean.'

The voice spoke to him a second time, 'Do not call anything impure that God has made clean.'

This happened three times, and immediately the sheet was taken back into heaven. (Acts 10. 9–16)

The apostle is commanded to eat food which his traditional Judaism had classified as unclean and so he instantly refuses. The vision has to be repeated twice more and it helps Peter to face up to his prejudices. So we can see that the vision experience did not rob him of his objectivity or rational sense even though he was undoubtedly emotionally upset.

Now it is important to understand this about visions because they are so closely paralleled by dreams. It is apparent that visions and dreams are, at some level, identical experiences. There are two quite common expressions occurring in the Old and New Testaments which compare visions and dreams. The first is 'vision of the night' and the second is 'the visions of my head'.[2] Interestingly enough, the visions in each of these cases concern the inner or personal reflections of the sleeper about his life or predicament. There is no message of proclamation for a nation or peoples concerning their conduct. Rather, the sleeper learns something about his own private situation and is challenged to do something appropriate. For Nebuchadnezzar it concerned God's challenge to his stubborn heart to acknowledge his dependence upon God for all his achievements (Dan. 4.10); for Paul the Apostle, it came as a confirmation that the difficulties he was having when preaching in the province of Asia indicated that he was to follow God's guidance to Macedonia (Acts 16. 6–10).

So we can say that dreams and visions are similar 'moments', when the sleeper reflects upon his personal situation. But whereas the former is usually the creation of the dreamer and provides an avenue for God to enter into dialogue with the individual, visions are given by God and the content is not dictated by the sleeper. And a further distinction between visions and dreams is that visions can happen whilst we are wide awake. This latter kind of vision has a totally different flavour from the sleeping vision and has to do with revelations of heaven, spiritual battles, prophetic challenges, and the end-times of judgement and global salvation.[3]

The Dream Routine

In the book of Job we find some clues to the reasons why we dream and how our dreams develop. The writer first lays down the fact that God wants to get in touch with us, only we refuse to hear the message. 'For God does speak – now one way, now another – though man may not perceive it. In a dream, in a vision of the night, when deep sleep falls on men as they slumber in their beds' (Job 33.14–15). So, if we fail to hear God's message to us whilst we are awake, he then takes the opportunity to come to us on the level of our dream life. This should make us really think about the fact that we are often more receptive to truth when we are asleep. I would go so far as to say that we are more honest when we are asleep than when we are awake. (Bear this in mind when we look later on at findings by counsellors and compare them with the biblical picture.)

However, if we fail to hear the dream message, then comes the development of the dream to the level of warnings or nightmares. 'When I think my bed will comfort me and my couch will ease my complaint, even then you frighten me with dreams and terrify me with visions ...' 'He may speak in their ears and terrify them with warnings ...' (Job 7.13–14; 33. 16). Yet there is a purpose even for nightmares; they are to help the dreamer change his life-style and save himself from possible harm: '. . . to turn man from wrong doing and keep him from pride, to preserve his soul from the pit, his life from perishing by the sword' (Job 33. 17–18). If the sleeper persists in ignoring such warnings from God to change his life, the final stage in this dream routine is that his life becomes sickened.

Whether or not this was the reason for Job's sufferings, it is certainly true that if we ignore what we find harmful for us we shall suffer the consequences. This dream process is confirmed by many contemporary psychologists, including Arthur Janov who says, in his book *The Primal Scream*, that many people are now in psychiatric care because they could not or would not pay attention to their dreams and especially their nightmares![4]

This dream routine can also be seen in the stories of Pharaoh's dreams which were interpreted by Joseph (Gen. 40–41) and also in the dream cycle of King Nebuchadnezzar (Dan. 2–4). In the case of Pharaoh, he had two dreams in sucession, both of which concerned an impending famine in the land. It is significant that Pharaoh awoke after each dream, as he was so troubled by what he had seen. I don't think that we are stretching the evidence to say that this seems to bear all the hallmarks of a nightmare. Pharoah was insistent that the dreams be correctly interpreted. According to Joseph, the reason for the persistence of the dreams was because 'the matter had been firmly decided by God, and God will do it soon' (Gen. 41.32). It seems then that God had been speaking to Pharoah and found a way to his mind by speaking into his dreams. Notice that Pharoah lost no time in following up the dream message once he had discovered it.

This was not the response of King Nebuchadnezzar when he learnt the meaning of his dreams. In this Bible account it seems that the king was too proud to listen to what God had been saying to him. So, when the same message came to him in his dreams, he was so disturbed that he could not get back to sleep. The king knew in his heart that there was a disturbing message in the dream, and he was determined to find it out (Dan. 2.1–12). Daniel introduced the interpretation with the words, 'As you lay in bed thoughts came of what would be hereafter' (Dan. 2.29). So before he drifted into sleep the king had been thinking over the future of his empire and rule. His dream reflected his thoughts in part; he saw a multi-metalled image of a man, each different metal representing different kingdoms. Yet his power was threatened by what he saw in his dream. God was taking action against him because of his pride. This was represented in the dream by the stone which had been cut out of the rock 'by no human hand'. 'And it smote the image on its feet of iron and clay, and broke them in pieces ... the whole image was smashed ... and it became like the chaff of the summer threshing floors, and the wind carried them away, so that not a trace of them could be found' (Dan. 2.34–5). The king's power and kingdom and even the memory of it – all was going to be obliterated by God. No wonder Nebuchadnezzar was upset!

Yet the amazing thing is that the king ignored God's warning to him. He promoted Daniel and thanked him for his help, and then he went on and in his stubborness seemed determined to challenge God and his own dreams. He built a giant statue of a man, and this time he went one better than his dream – he built it all of gold. Soon a second dream followed. This time it was of a great tree which was to be reduced to nothing more than a bare stump (Dan. 4.4–16). Once again Daniel was summoned as interpreter and the message was a warning to the king; if he persisted in his pride and ambition, then

God would reduce him to living off the land like an animal. Again the king ignored the message and, according to the dream routine already outlined, he was inflicted with illness – insanity in this case. It was only when the king humbled himself and acknowledged the God who had challenged him in his dreams, that he recovered his faculties and returned to normal life, this time with praise for the God of heaven in his heart.

So we have established a pattern of dreaming as far as the biblical picture goes. God speaks to us in waking life and then continues to communicate through dreams which intensify in feeling if we ignore the message. The final stage of the process is the physical or emotional stress that comes when we repress the truth from ourselves.

Dream Power

According to the Bible, the ability to understand dreams, as well as having dreams through which God speaks, is to be in a position of spiritual power. Both Joseph and Daniel are recorded as saying that their ability to interpret is a gift of God. Daniel says to God, 'Praise be to the name of God for ever and ever ... He reveals deep and hidden things; he knows what lies in darkness, and light dwells with him ... You have given me wisdom and power ... You have made known to us the dream of the king' (Dan. 2.19–23).[5]

Spiritual power comes from being able to know the word of God for others, and this is precisely what some dream interpretations in the Bible conveyed. It rocketed Daniel and Joseph into positions of prominence and power within their communities. Prophets were respected because they too received God's word. It should not surprise us then to learn that they were, quite respectfully, also called 'dreamers'. 'If there is a prophet among you, I the Lord will speak to him in a dream' (Num. 12.6).[6]

When the prophet Jeremiah castigated the false prophets of the day he referred to their spiritual resources of visions and dreams (Jer. 23.25,27). Even the call to be a prophet began for some with the experience of a vision or dream: Moses was transfixed by the vision of the burning bush (Exod. 3.2ff); Samuel as a young man was having a restless sleep when suddenly God spoke to him (1 Sam. 3.1ff): Elisha, worried whether he was really called to the prophetic ministry, lost all his doubts when he saw the vision of his mentor Elijah going up to heaven on a chariot (2 Kings 2.12ff);

Isaiah was praying in the temple at a time of national mourning when he suddenly had a vision of the glory of God in the land of sinners (Isa. 6.1ff). Even Jesus received encouragement and strength from his transfiguration vision of Moses and Elijah on the mountain top (Mark 9.1ff).

It is surprising and challenging to read of significant times of guidance, deliverance, encouragement and healing which have hinged on an objective response to dreams. One of the greatest promises ever given to an individual was through a dream: God promised Abraham to make of his descendants a great nation which would include a deliverer, and to do this he came to Abraham as he slept (Gen. 15.1). This promise of God's blessing for a nation was repeated in a dream to the refugee Jacob as he slept outside Bethel one night. It was during a dream that King Solomon was challenged by God to ask for what he really wanted as the newly crowned monarch, and it was in his sleep that he worshipped his God and asked for the gifts of wisdom and understanding. This dream encounter led to a time of unparalleled peace and prosperity in the life of Israel (1 Kings 3.5–14.).

Consider the very real deliverance that was given to the infant Jesus through the warning dreams given to the wise men not to report the whereabouts of the birth to Herod. This only delayed the inevitable, but it gained precious time allowing the family to flee to safety in Egypt. The guidance and warning was repeated through dreams to Joseph, when he was told that the old king had died but that as Archelaus ruled in Judea it would be better to go to Nazareth (Matt. 2.12–13,19,22). Incidentally, the Greek word used here for warning is 'chrematisthentes' which means 'to give response to those consulting an oracle'. The same word occurs in Luke 2.26, where it is used in the sense of revealing to Simeon some truth from God about his life. In saying this, it seems then that the gospel is underlining this use of dream as a vehicle for divine revelation.

We have already mentioned the guidance given to Paul concerning the direction of his evangelistic missions, and it is worth reminding ourselves of the momentous consequences this had for bringing the gospel on to European soil. The taking of the gospel outside the comparatively minor Jewish world in which it had been born was a direct consequence of the vision which Peter had on the roof-top in Joppa.

And what of the tremendous implications of obeying a vision for an unknown disciple called Ananias, as well as for the apostle Paul

himself! Ananias had a vision in which God told him what had
happened to Paul on the Damascus road and that he, Ananias, was
to go and lay hands on him and pray for his healing (Acts 10.10–18).
He obeyed, and the result was that a man was converted, healed of
his blindness and then filled with spirit. Paul himself later testifies to
the great significance of the experience and speaks of the call of God
that came upon his life at this time to go and preach the gospel.
He sums up his response in those immortal words, 'I was not
disobedient to the heavenly vision' (Acts 26.19).

So we can see that the range of application of dreams is wide and
varied. This is to say nothing about the teaching role of dreams and
visions in the Bible, the most notable being that of the Revelation,
where John was shown so many pictures of God in action in
times present and future. Yet we must not conclude this section on
spiritual power and dreams without some words on renewal. It was
the prophet Joel who spoke in his prophecy of a time of spiritual
renewal which was to come, and one of the signs of this time would
be that 'your young men shall see visions and your old men dream
dreams' (Joel 2.28). These very words were repeated on the Day of
Pentecost by Peter who was confirming that the promised day of
power had now come. The impact of these words must not be lost
to us; whereas in former days the experience of spiritual power in
any form was limited to the chosen few, in the latter days such
power was going to be made available to all. Yet, sadly, it seems that
the Christian Church after the times of the apostles began to lose
interest in dreams and visions and as a consequence, I believe, lost
some of its power to know God in a personal and immediate sense.
It is no accident that in the modern experience of spiritual renewal,
whether it be charismatic or otherwise, one of the features beginning to emerge is a revived interest in visions and dreams. I am
convinced that the Holy Spirit wishes to teach us to reopen these
personal doors of self-awareness and to allow dreams to become a
vehicle for God to speak to us as he wills. The basic thrust of
the Bible's understanding of dreams is that they are a normal experience whereby the dreamer is reflecting upon his own life and
circumstances. Yet they are also channels by which God's power
and presence are released into lives, and in this way they have been
used to change the direction of nations and individuals alike. This
has only happened however when the dreamer listened to his dream
message and acted sensitively upon it.

3 Twentieth-Century Dreaming

We shall now look at some of the findings of modern dream researchers and see if these support what we have discovered from the biblical evidence.

There has been a revolution in attitudes towards dreaming in the last fifty years. In the centuries following the establishment of the Christian Church there developed a scepticism about the usefulness of dreams, and they were largely consigned to the realm of the fanciful and fringe interests of minority groups.[1] The tide of major interest in dreams began to turn with the publication of Sigmund Freud's work entitled *The Interpretation of Dreams*, which appeared in 1900. This sparked off a study of dreams that was largely confined to the students and practitioners of psychoanalysis. In a moment we shall examine some of their basic findings. The popular interest in dreams really got under way with the work of two researchers in the United States, Nathaniel Kleitman of the Department of Physiology at the University of Chicago and William Dement of Mount Sinai Hospital in New York.

Kleitman monitored the eye movements of sleepers, and he discovered that each person had a cycle of sleeping which repeated itself about four or five times during a normal eight-hour period of rest. The end of each cycle was characterized by rapid eye movements (REM). What was fascinating about all this was that the eye movements were binocularly synchronous; that is, both eyes moved in the same direction and at the same speed. Even blind people had REM sleep! Ann Faraday, in her book *Dream Power*, has said that the REM periods resembled the sleeper watching something like a Shakespearean tragedy. At first the movement was quite steady, and then suddenly there was a rapid burst of activity before the events settled down again. Eighty per cent of those sleepers awakened during REM sleep were able to recall their dreams quite vividly, whereas the majority of those who woke up during non-REM sleep could only relate their dreams in vague detail. So for the first time in history it became possible to know exactly when a person is dreaming in some detail.

The next interesting development in dream discovery was the

dream deprivation experiments of William Dement. He discovered
that those people deprived of REM sleep became highly agitated
and could not continue the experiment beyond three days. On the
other hand, those deprived of non-REM sleep, whilst denied the
same length of sleep as the first group, were not so upset and could
have continued the process indefinitely. What this proved was that
without REM sleep, and its vivid dream content, we suffer. So
purely from a physiological aspect it can be said that 'dreams are
good for you'.[2]

By examining the dream content and comparing this with certain
external stimuli it was easily concluded that the dreamer is the sole
architect of his or her dreams. Compare the following example;

> Thirty seconds before waking the subject from a REM period, I had
> sprinkled cold water on her hand, which was lying on the bed covers.
> When awakened and asked to report what had been passing through her
> mind just prior to waking, she reported: 'I had just jumped on a train as
> it started to move off, and was feeling relieved I had managed to catch it.
> I was just lighting a cigarette when I felt water on my hand and saw that
> the rain was coming in through the window. I got up to shut it, when I
> heard the carriage door open from the other end, and a man in a chef's
> hat came in and sat down. He pretended to read his paper, but I could
> feel him looking at me out of the corner of his eye. I muttered something
> about the weather but he didn't answer. I got panicky and edged my way
> to the door. I could do it only when he wasn't looking. I kept sitting and
> standing up, trying to get out, when you woke me up.'[3]

It is important to grasp this simple but profound truth; the
dreamer writes the script for his own dreams. He may incorporate
external sounds and influences into his dream but they do not
initiate the dream. The question which we need to raise now is:
'Why do we dream in the first place?' Are there some personal
reasons why we need the dream? Why, for example, do we wish to
frighten ourselves with nightmares? As a first step toward answer-
ing these questions, we shall consider the theories of some
psychologists about dreams and compare their basic assumptions
with those that are presented in the Bible.

Sigmund Freud

No proper assessment of the reasons for dreaming would be
complete without looking at the ideas of Sigmund Freud. For him
there was no transcendent God who could communicate with his
creation through dreams. Man was another species of animal, and

there was no difference to be found between human decision and animal impulse or instinct. To put it simply, man's basic dilemma was not some cosmic fall by which he had been separated from his God, but only that he or she had lost touch with themselves. Freud brought to public attention the whole area of the unconscious mind which motivated and shaped the public behaviour of the person. He went on to identify this area with the repressed and often threatening aspects of our animal instincts.

To understand Freud's ideas about dreaming we need to examine briefly his beliefs about human behaviour. He saw this arising from three sources: the 'id', or unconscious, which is concerned with the discharge of the basic drives of a man's energy and tensions; the conscious mind, or 'ego', which regulates interaction with the surrounding environment; finally, the 'superego', which represents the moral demands of the community. These three elements live in an uneasy tension with each other, kept in balance by the ego through a process of displacement whereby the more threatening and destructive forces reappear in the form of jokes, dreams or repression itself. So this brings us to Freud's whole ethos of dreams; it is a means by which the individual can give room to his fantasies and fears which would be totally unacceptable in waking life. Therefore for Freud, the architect of the dream is the unconscious mind itself. There is a remarkable similarity in his thought to that of Plato who regarded dreams as the place where the bestial side of man could safely vent its anger without fear of damage. However, Freud goes further by saying that the dream symbols are there in order to disguise the real meaning of the dream lest the message alarm the sleeper and awaken him prematurely. In his celebrated book he writes, 'In this house on July 24th, 1895 the secret of dreams was revealed to Dr Sigmund Freud.'[4]

The secret he had discovered was that the purpose of dreaming is 'wish-fulfilment'. No matter what the dream message – one's own death, violence done to a loved one – it is all wish-fulfilment. However, Freud went on to distinguish between two layers of dreaming: the manifest element, which is linked to the immediate events in the life of the dreamer, and the latent, which is connected with the more ancient and basic elements of human nature. It is the symbols of the dream which have distorted the real or latent part of the dream. So it seems that the sleeper behaves exactly as he does when awake in fleeing from his less acceptable drives. Therefore, a dream needs to be taken apart in order to reach the latent kernel which is waiting to be retrieved.

Freud's insistence on this theory often led him into rather strained attempts at dream interpretation to say the least. For example, when a patient produced a dream that seemingly contradicted his theory he would respond by saying, 'Thus it was her wish that I might be wrong, and her dream showed that wish fulfilled.'[5] Again, when a lawyer friend dreamed that he had lost all his (legal) suits, certainly not a wish, Freud interpreted this to mean that the lawyer wished that he, Freud, be disgraced.

A further step in achieving the inner dream message came by the principle of free association; each aspect of the dream was taken to see what it conjured up in the mind and feelings, and herein lay the real clues to the meaning of the dream. This process included the dissecting of words in order to release further clues. Freud interpreted the words 'Ger Italia' (let us go to Italy) as genitalia. Even in words, Freud maintained, the forbidden desires were present 'in code'. These forbidden desires were largely sexual in nature, but it needs to be understood that Freud often used this term to refer to the drive for emotional fulfilment.

Freud also pointed out that there are two kinds of dream symbols, those culled from former times and which are passed on through the community in which people are born and those which are culled from the private fears and fantasies of the dreamer. The first category are easily identified and reflect the metaphors, jokes and religious ideas of each culture, whereas the second can only be identified through free association and a knowledge of symbols related to sexual imagery. In this connection Freud produced a long list of items which he said represented the sexual organs. This is, to say the least, a very arbitrary approach to symbols and is more akin to the dream dictionaries of the ancient Middle Eastern cultures.

To summarize our brief review of Freud on dreams, we see that the prime value of his work lies in the fact that he firmly linked the process of dreaming to that of the unconscious mind at work and play. He was the first to establish that sleep is not a coma-like condition but an active process of a mind awake. He emphasized that dreams relate to events both immediate and from the buried past of the dreamer. He also represented dreaming as an attempt to come to terms with the emotional tensions of the individual's present approach to life. However, he privatized the ability to interpret dreams by making it the preserve of the specialized counsellor, and he regarded the whole purpose of symbols to be one of distortion and disguising of the dream message. His successors were to disagree strongly with this use of symbols and, on the contrary, to regard them as open disclosures of what concerned the sleeping mind.

Carl Gustav Jung

Carl Jung was a disciple and close friend of Freud, but later they parted company as Jung disagreed with Freud's exclusive interpretation of psychological symbols as being of a psycho-sexual nature. This disagreement revealed itself largely in their differing approaches to dream interpretation. Freud saw dream symbols as a device to distort or disguise the true dream message, whereas Jung saw dreams as an integral part of human behaviour which harboured no intention to deceive but rather to express something, much in the way that a plant reveals its blooms when it is allowed to grow. Jung saw dreams as a compensating factor which made up for what was lacking in waking life; they served as a warning of need, a call for attention as well as a statement of desire by the sleeper:

> The dream gives a true picture of the subjective state, while the conscious mind denies that this state exists, or recognizes it only grudgingly. It has no respect for ... conjectures, or for the patient's views as to how things should be, but simply tells how the matter stands. It is the way of dreams to give us more than we ask. They not only allow us insight into the causes of psycho-neuroses, but afford a prognosis as well.[6]

So it seems that the unconscious mind actually battles against the conscious mind sometimes in order to give a voice to the as yet unexpressed feelings of the dreamer. Jung also disagreed with Freud's idea of the manifest and latent dream. The dream itself is a whole and comes as a practical and important hint showing which direction the unconscious mind wishes to go. The term that Jung used at this point was 'individuation', and by this he meant that working with our dreams helps us to reintegrate the whole of our personality and so become more complete persons.

Jung said that the symbols of our dreams carry messages from the instinctive part of our nature to the rational mind. He described the symbols of dreams as representing the three elements that make up human nature. First there are the symbols that refer to our 'persona' – the roles that we play in society, in our jobs, our hobbies and sports; they essentially refer to how we think others see our public face. Behind and beneath the persona lies the 'shadow' – that part of us which is often denied in public to others and often to ourselves. Consider for example the following dream account:

A man dreamt that he was being walked along the road by his father who had him on a dog's lead although he walked upright. They went into a china shop and as they were standing by the counter, a huge black bull came crashing through the window and began to wreck everything in the shop.

When this dream was discussed it was seen that the dreamer felt that his father was leading him a dog's life; indeed his father had dominated his life. In the dream he had also felt really good and quite powerful when the bull came crashing into the shop, whereas his father was completely upset at this mess. The dreamer saw this as a part of him that wanted to rebel against his father's ordering of his life. He was in fact surprised and heartened by his ability to feel aggressive and saw this as a bid for freedom to be in control of his own life. So here the shadow part of his life was being given a voice in his dream.

Deeper still than this is the collective unconscious. By this Jung meant the sum of primordial images of age-old experience which we inherit from the human past and from the universal spirit. Jung believed that these symbols were mainly religious by nature. In one classic passage in his book, *Modern Man in Search of a Soul* he writes:

> Among all my patients in the second half of life ... there has not been one whose problem in the last resort was not that of finding a religious outlook on life. It is safe to say that every one of them felt ill because he had lost that which the living religions of every age have given to their followers, and none of them has been really healed who did not regain his religious outlook.[7]

This is not to say that Jung fixed his ideas to the doctrines of any religion in particular; he was referring to the innate need of mankind to worship and experience the sacred. So we see that for Jung, dreams allow people to tap into their whole being, and at the root of this is the need to re-own the sacred. By listening to the dream picture we begin to learn more about ourselves and so enter into another step of personal growth and wholeness.

Thus Jung takes us another step along the trail of our understanding of dreams. It was he who emphasized that the dream is an open message from the dreamer to himself. He also underlined that by working with our dreams we learn to keep in touch with all of our feelings, conscious and unconscious. He it was who saw in the dream symbols something of our neglected spirituality which he was intent on resurrecting. Finally, it was Jung who brought dream interpretation back into the orbit of the dreamer himself. He encouraged people to meditate upon their dreams until they got an answer that 'felt right'.

Calvin S. Hall

Calvin Hall was a noted dream researcher and, in the words of Ann Faraday, he and Fritz Perls 'have taken the whole subject out of the consulting room and into the market place and made dream interpretation a possibility for all of us in everyday life'.[8] Hall, like Jung before him, became dissatisfied with Freud's approach to dream interpretation and pointed out that Freud's findings were based entirely upon working with his own patients. Hall wanted to sample the dreams of ordinary people who were not undergoing psychiatric help and so gain an insight into 'normal' dreams. He recorded people's dreams in the natural surroundings of their own homes and analysed no less than 10,000 dreams.

Hall's conclusions can be found in his major book called *The Meaning of Dreams*.[9] He discovered that most dreams were concerned with the individual's ordinary surroundings, although not usually concerned with work, study or commercial transactions. Most of the dream characters were people with whom the dreamer had day-to-day contact. In other words the main preoccupation of dreams was the present and surrounding experiences of the dreamer. They reflected a person's worries, about the sort of person he was, how others saw him and he them, and what the world itself was going to do to him. Hall agreed with Jung that the symbolic language of dreams was a condensed form of expression which, once learned, can show many aspects of thinking that escape notice during the day. He gave four basic rules of dream interpretation:

1. The dream is the creation of the dreamer's own mind and tells him how he sees himself, others, his world and his impulses. It should never be read as a guide to objective reality but as a picture of how these things appear to us.
2. The dreamer is responsible for everything that appears in the dream. However terrible the dream, he must first have thought of it.
3. A dreamer usually has more than one conception of himself. There is usually a different picture to suit the mood of the moment of the dream.
4. A dream ought not to be interpreted without consulting other

dreams in the same series. Very often the meaning of one dream will shed light on other, associated dreams.

Calvin Hall helps us to understand the dream as a personal document to oneself. The meaning of the dream is found by the process of association of ideas. Themes which occur in the dream are to be compared with other attitudes or fears which they arouse and are therefore to be confronted. The objective element is played down in favour of the subjective. His emphasis upon accountability for the dream enables a person really to tackle their own dreaming, and in this way Hall has indeed helped to bring dream interpretation back into use for the common man.

Frederick (Fritz) Perls

Perls' methods, known as '*Gestalt*' (from the German word for 'a complete pattern'), have become part of a major popular movement in America: the Human Potential Movement, which includes encounter groups, sensory awareness workshops and the like; they are all geared towards promoting personal growth. Therapy consists of looking for the 'here and now' problems of personal behaviour. There is to be no concentration upon tracing back to some infantile trauma as is the case in psychoanalysis. Perls looks out for such things as facial expressions, the tone of voice, posture, gestures and reactions to other people as clues to where the present pain may lie.

He sees dreams as an added bonus to healing; they are the royal road to integration. Dreams are an existential message telling us exactly where we are in relation to ourselves, to others and to the world around us. What Perls seeks to do is uncover the various messages within the dream and bring them together to from a whole picture of the person; in doing this any lost or hidden parts of the person's present level of awareness are re-owned. This in itself is healing.

The following is an outline of the method Perls suggests for working with dreams:

1. Retell the dream in the first person and, whilst doing so, get in touch with the feelings that are connected with the dream pictures. Look out for facial expressions, etc.

2. When two dream images meet in dialogue, then employ the 'empty chair' model. By moving from his own chair to the empty one and back the dreamer can give a voice to the

different messages within his dream. Expression of any strong emotions which may come out during this time is encouraged as, according to Perls, this helps confront any buried fears and reduces anxiety.

3. If the person has difficulty in playing the role of any particular part of his dream, then this is an indication that a buried part of the person's attitude to life is being touched. What is encouraged here is basically that the individual gets tough with himself and so begin to own as his, the unwanted elements and takes authority over himself. This is the road to wholeness according to Perls.[10]

Perls has had a big influence on such ministries as 'the healing of the memories', since many have seen this process as one which can be 'christianized'. It is certainly true that the Scriptures point out that in Jesus we have a saviour who can enter into the feelings of our weaknesses (Heb. 4.15 AV). Therefore, by allowing Jesus access to our dreams and focusing upon the feelings there, we begin to experience the integration of our feelings with our faith. This process, of bringing to the surface the repressed hurts and feelings of our lives, corresponds to the growth in Christ and walking in the light which is necessary for every Christian.

Ann Faraday

Ann Faraday represents for us the latest stage in dream development from a psychotherapeutic point of view. With Hall and Perls she demythologizes the role of the specialist-counsellor-cum-dream-interpreter from that of a secular diviner to a caring individual with the minimum of training. In her view a dream reflects how the individual sees his world and it is sometimes more frank than his waking description would be; this is because dreaming is an opportunity to pay proper attention to factors ignored at 'gut' level when awake. However, Faraday, like Perls before her, does not support the idea that in dreams the unconscious comes to the surface. Rather, she sees a continuity from waking to sleeping, and dreams as an attempt to reconcile what has not received proper attention during the day. This would certainly underline the biblical experience of dreaming, where God has spoken to the dreamer about matters which they have ignored when awake. Faraday also states that dream symbols and pictures need to be treated objectively if possible. In other words, if I dream of someone I know, such as my wife or my minister, then I am to ask myself what it is that I feel or think about that person at this moment. If nothing comes to mind then, and only then should a person proceed to see if the person represents an aspect of their own lives or situation.

Where Faraday goes further than others before her is in the way that she employs the dream itself as counsellor. She encourages her clients, when in need of further counsel and when therapy has so far proven ineffective, to sit down and in a calm frame of mind to ask their dreams to come to their aid. Exactly the same method is employed if one has a dream which is difficult to interpret; ask for another dream to interpret the first one and so remove the deadlock. This is what she calls 'dream power', and by this she is not speaking of some hidden or occultic power but using it merely as a term for the unique ability of dreams to reach in and enlighten the nature of our feelings and problems when other conventional methods have failed. The following is a prayer which she suggests using:

> Thank you, dream power, for the dream I had last night. I feel it's an important dream, but despite all my efforts, I'm still unable to get the message. Please send me another dream tonight putting the same message in a way I can understand. I'll make extra effort to remember my dreams, and I promise to write down anything you send immediately on waking. Thanks.[11]

This exercise may seem like praying to the false god of the sleeping self, but for Faraday it is simply verbalizing a desire to get in touch with all the levels of one's life. Yet as Christians, who believe in a loving Father God who has given sleep as one of his gifts to his children, surely we can ask the Father to use our dream life to help us walk with him? Therefore, I suggest the following as a prayer for those who want to invite the Lord of all life to use their sleep life as a means of grace:

> Heavenly Father, I thank you that waking or sleeping, you are the God of my salvation. Father, I come to you for more healing and invite you to show me more of myself as you desire. I give to you my sleep for this night and ask that, through Jesus Christ my Lord, you will grant me to know more truth through my dreams and that by listening to them I shall be free to serve you more, through Christ my Lord. Amen.

Faraday challenges not only Christians, but non-Christians also, to respect their dreams and not only to listen to their message but to act upon them sensitively. She charges the Church with neglect of so great an opportunity of communication with God and for personal learning.

What then can we learn as Christians from this brief survey of dreams from a modern counselling point of view? Are there any parallels or are the contrasts too great to be of any value to those of the Christian faith?

The basic message is that dreams are not the nonsense wanderings of a mind too filled with cheese and wine from the night before! The modern psychologists we have considered all agree that dreams contain messages and reflections of the dreamer's own life which, for one reason or another, he has not listened to properly. This exactly matches the dream routine we have outlined in the previous chapter. They agree also that by giving a voice to the dream the dreamer actually benefits from the process in terms of his own emotional and mental well-being. Daniel's biography of Nebuchadnezzar illustrated this truth some centuries before them! They all agree too that to some degree dreams reveal things that have been hidden from the dreamer, sometimes by the dreamer himself. Daniel writes about a sovereign God who confronts the dreamer with truth which he has been denying himself when awake, and goes on to describe the consequences which are likely to follow. They are all more or less in agreement that the symbols of each dream make sense to the dreamer because they are culled from his own world and culture: a little time set aside to work with one's dream symbols soon brings to light what they represent for us.

On the basis of these observations it seems that what is needed next is a step of faith. Just as it is the duty of each Christian to offer to God all that he learns of life and nature, so too he can offer to God his dream life and so reopen a door through which he can learn his personality as God has chosen to create him and also provide another channel through which God can communicate with him. In the next few chapters we shall explore more deeply how we can grow spiritually through a biblical approach to dreams and so appreciate the spiritual power of dreaming.

4 Opening the Dream Door

Working with dreams has led me into some interesting places. As a result of giving two Lent talks on the subject, a church in Derbyshire invited me to attend their annual garden party in order to offer dream interpretation to any who were interested. I do not see myself at all as an interpreter and prefer to regard myself as one who works with other people as they explore their dreams, but I decided to take up the offer and trust that the Lord was 'in this'.

On this particular occasion a lady came to me and shared a dream in which she saw herself as a child who was depressed and disappointed at the way her hopes had been dashed. I asked her if she had in fact had a great disappointment. She took me to one side and said that her husband, who was a doctor, was then in the advanced stages of multiple sclerosis and had to be pushed around in a wheelchair. Further sharing revealed that she had slowly been building up resentment towards God and her husband that this had happened, and that her husband had not been healed, nor his condition improved, through the many prayers of the church. However, she had not dared to utter a word of these feelings but had bottled them all up inside her; as a consequence she got very moody with her husband, whom she loved. After a while she came to see that the child in her dream related to her more creative and zestful spirit and that she was hoping to have more time to do things for herself now that her children had grown up and left home. Having a handicapped husband had put an end to her hopes. She immediately decided to go over to her husband and apologize, tactfully she hoped, for her bouts of moodiness and explain the reasons for it.

Later on that day I met up with both of them and they were grateful for the opportunity that had come their way to confront the feelings buried beneath the surface of their relationship. Now they felt they had some solid ground from which to face the future and its implications together. Opening the door for the dream message to be given a hearing had proved a step forward in their relationship. For anyone, but especially for the Christian, facing and acting upon truth will always bring us an opportunity for spiritual growth. This is surely the testimony of Scripture; as men were given the message of the dreams so they were presented with an opportunity to come to God and seek his will for what they should do next. Pharoah obeyed God's word to him, Nebuchadnezzar rebelled, but both had had their dreams interpreted and so had a choice to make.

In November 1985, at the time my first booklet on dreams was published,[1] I received an invitation from BBC Radio Leicester to join their Crosstalk programme to give a one-hour live phone-in on dreams. Whilst not wanting to appear a freak or a guru of dreams, I felt that this too was an opportunity from God. So I duly agreed and the programme went on the air. Of the many dreams which were relayed to the studio, one concerned a lady who had recently lost her father. She told me the following dream:

> I was asleep in bed when I suddenly awoke. There was my father dressed in top hat and tails and looking really good. He smiled at me and sat on the end of the bed for a while. I was very pleased to see him in such good shape. Then he said that it was time for him to go, and with ease he seemed to glide out of the room.

This lady told me that her father had died of cancer over a year before and that this was the first time she could remember dreaming of him. She wanted to know why this was so and what was the dream about. I checked out with her about her relationship with her father which was very loving and that she had really missed him since he died. When I began to ask her why she felt good in the dream she replied by saying that he looked so smart and happy, and that as he loved old-time dancing it seemed fitting that he should wear those clothes. I then suggested that perhaps the dream was telling her that she had now reached the stage in her life when she could stop 'hanging on' to her father and resume her own life more fully. The top hat and tails was her way of saying that wherever her father was, he was in the right place, according to her own feelings, and that this was good. The smile from her father was her way of saying, 'He understands, it is OK for me to get on with my own life now.' She immediately acknowledged that this was absolutely true and that her life was now getting back to normal and she was feeling her old self again. She had in fact only just begun to talk about her father without it feeling painful, and her dream seemed to confirm this.

What was interesting about this was that a few days after the radio broadcast the leader of a local bereavement group called at the house to say that she and some other members of this group had been helped by the comments on the above dream. They asked me to go and speak to their group, which I did, and this resulted in counselling and praying with a number of them who wanted to receive God's peace and comfort in their time of loss and separation. Some were concerned that they had not dreamed about their loved ones and asked if something was wrong with them. I replied by saying that as their organization provided plenty of space for them to talk out their hurt feelings, they had no need to repeat this in sleep. The time would eventually come when all the need for talking would be done and that would be a more likely time for their dreams to include such material. The effect of all this sharing was that many of these people began to respect their dreams and appeciate their function. A door of understanding had opened for them, and it was a dream door at that.

Dreams are like Parables

So it can be seen that dreams pick up some of the thoughts and feelings which correspond to what we are currently experiencing but which have not necessarily been given proper attention. By giving these feelings a voice (i.e. by listening to the dream message) we get in touch with more that is going on inside us, and this provides us with an opportunity to go forward in our lives. It is almost as if each dream has a basic punch-line which it is trying to state. By seeing the punch-line we take a further step along the road of meaning.

Now it is in this respect that dreams and parables are similar experiences. It was F.F. Bruce who said that a parable is a story with a kick like a mule. There may well be other material in the story, all of which may be relevant, but the 'kick' is the main message to be grasped. Jesus gave some of his teaching in parables so that those who really wanted to learn his truths might see beyond the immediate 'picture' and grasp the kernel of teaching within. The merely curious would only hear a story and so would remain blind to the teaching offered.[2] The dream is a personal parable we have written to ourselves in order to send a basic message which we have been blind to in waking life. Too often the dreamer is bemused by the picture and its symbols and so doesn't bother to look into the dream and pick out the bottom line of the message contained within. The punch-line is there if only we give ourselves a little time to discover it.

Another parallel between dream and parable is that of motivation.
Jesus told his stories as an aid to encourage his hearers to step
into truth that would give life. They could see themselves as that
prodigal son coming to his senses and returning in repentance to his
father, or as the lost sheep whom Jesus had come to rescue from
certain death. They were stories told with the intention of creating a
response of faith. So with dreams, they call us to move on in life in
accordance with their basic message. Granted that most of the time
the message may not appear to be of outstanding importance, nonetheless it is a message we think important enough to relay back to
ourselves whilst asleep. Therefore the message needs at least to be
acknowledged.

This is especially true of nightmares and recurring dreams. If we
accept that we ourselves basically write the scripts to our dreams,
then why is it that we wish to frighten ourselves? Now one of the
most obvious common denominators of all nightmares is that, when
the dreadful deed or frightening 'thing' of our dream is about to
pounce upon us, we 'bail out of the dream'. We wake up. This is
because the dream material contains some 'unfinished business'
taking place within our lives that is too painful or is buried too
deep within our feelings for us to consider at that moment. This
explains why the dream is so abruptly terminated. The dreamer is
able to relate the dream itself and the fact that it was frightening, but
that is usually as far as it goes. The feelings of fear remain to cause
upset. For a Christian facing such dreams there is the need of a faith
response in order to confront the 'punch-line' within the dream and
so move into a further opportunity for growth. Surely there can be
no proper healing of our lives if we have not first 'owned up' to the
issues and needs contained within. Once we have accepted responsibility for each and any part of our lives, then and only then, are we
in a position to come into the light and seek God's help.

So what I am advocating is that this process is also true for dream
material. As we listen to the basic message of our dreams and
respond in faith to what they describe about our outlook on our
circumstances, then let us come before God and share with him the
issues of the moment and seek his help and guidance. By accepting
this response to dreams we open up a door for them to be used
for our growth in self-understanding, for bringing healing to our
emotions and inner lives, for making them the basis of sharing
our feelings and needs and so promoting furthur oppurtunities for
development of fellowship and ministry among Christians.

All these areas in which dreams may be applied will be more fully explored in the following chapters.

Discerning the Dream Message

This is not the place to enter into elaborate discussions about dream symbols and their meanings, but it would be helpful here to outline one or two clues about the essential thrust or the direction in which a dream may be pointing.

Feelings

A major clue to what the dream is saying is to look out for the feelings contained within it. They can save us from a lot of needless misdirection. For example, consider the following dream told by a woman who was in training for ordination in the Church of England:

> I was about sixteen years old and back at my old secondary school. I was with some of the girls from my form and we were having a lesson but also sitting in our swimsuits beside a pool. Then a young man came walking by but he was covered completely in black and we could not see his face.

When I asked her what was the significance of the man in black and the fact that his face could not be seen, she immediately replied that she thought it was obviously the Devil and that he was there to tempt her. But when I asked her how she felt at that moment her tone changed and she said that she felt quite excited and attracted to the man. A further checking of the facts revealed that at that time there was a new teacher in her school and he was both young and attractive. However, try as some of the girls did, they could not get the teacher to talk about himself and they were 'in the dark' (her words not mine) about what he was really like. As soon as she said these words a look of recognition dawned upon her face, she intuitively knew that her man in black was not the Devil but the teacher to whom she had been momentarily attracted. It also transpired that she was feeling in the dark about her future career, and so the dream served to illustrate her mixed feelings about going into the ministry. She was certainly attracted to the ministry but was unsure about how it would affect her personal life.

Another person had a nightmare of being pursued by a cloaked figure and thought that perhaps this was about some deep-seated fear of the unknown. But when she checked out the feelings of the dream she was a little puzzled as the figure was wanting to help her and was hurt at her response. It turned out that the dream related to an operation that went wrong and that there was still a lot of unresolved anger in her life about the standard of medical treatment she had received. The patient had continued to rebuff those who had tried to help her and she confessed to having, right up to the time of relating the dream, an aversion to calling in a doctor or going to the dentist. The dream feeling accurately reflected this ambivalence and, by facing up to the clues presented, she was able to work out the anger and come to a greater harmony within her life.

So feelings offer a very real and positive indication as to the direction of the dream message.

Everyday events

Secondly, it is just as well to check out recent and familiar events in your life to see if they match up to the dream itself. Very often the symbols of a dream will relate to the individual's everyday circumstances. Joseph dreamed about sheaves of grain, the sun, moon and stars – familiar things to a herdsman who would spend many hours out in the open field with his cattle. Often he would sleep under the open heavens. The butler he met in jail dreamt of the grapevine and pressing grapes into the cup of the king; the baker dreamed of bread trays which he would often carry upon his head.

In 1986 I was one of the tutors at a course on introducing pastoral counselling. One of the other tutors, who was a lay chaplain at a nearby hospital and the wife of an Anglican minister, shared a recent dream she had had. Essentially, it focused upon some tensions she was experiencing with some Christian friends and acquaintances. What was fascinating was that the dream took the form of exploring some of the rooms of a house in a wood. The house was still being built and there was no roof as yet. After working with her dream I asked if there was indeed a house or building which was incomplete which figured in her life at all. She replied by saying that the church which she belonged to was then having scaffolding erected around it in preparation for extension and repairs to be done.

So this dream used the current issue of the church building being under repair and incomplete as the starting base for reflecting the punch-line of her life (the house) needing to change and be properly complete. Just as changes and adjustments had to be made to the church, so the dreamer felt the need to change and adjust her life-style and relations with others. This dream will be shared more fully in chapter 6 on dreams and healing.

Some months ago a friend wrote about a dream in a letter to me and asked if I could help him understand it.

> In his dream he was crossing the river Mersey in a boat going from Liverpool to Birkenhead. As the boat drew close to the landing-stage he began to feel anxious as to whether he would make it ashore, and it was then that he noticed a small fish flapping about inside the boat. He did nothing about the fish but was just able to get ashore.

In my reply to him I asked if there was anything in his life which was consciously bothering him. He replied by saying that he was thinking of changing his job and wasn't sure if this was what God wanted him to do. But by way of introduction he had said that in his present job he was in the habit of going over to Liverpool and back on the Mersey ferry boats! So travelling to work by boat supplied the immediate setting for the dream, and when I asked him to reflect on how he felt in his dream about the fish out of the water he wrote back saying that this fitted into how he felt about changing his job; he wasn't sure if he could cope with the change. So by reviewing the recent events we get an indication of where the dream has arisen and a clue as to where it is leading.

Childhood experiences

A further help to discovering the dream direction is to gather some biographical details, particularly childhood experiences and feelings. This will provide an insight into your hopes and hurts and also information about major moments which may still colour and shape how you see life today.

For example, there was Ann, a married woman in her early thirties, who came to talk about some of her nightmares as part of the counselling we were sharing. By far the most familiar material in these dreams was that of houses in which she felt pursued by two men who seemed to glare at her, though they did not attempt to harm her in any way. During discussion prior to working through the dreams she told me that, until she was about eighteen years old, she had lived in a number of houses in which she never felt safe. She could remember as a little child being left with her grandmother in one of these houses, and she recalled that the windows and doors never shut properly and consequently she never felt safe or protected there. Another memory which she had shared was of feeling that she had been put on show by her parents and was not allowed to be herself in front of others. Consequently, her two uncles especially had always been in the habit of making fun at her expense. It became clear that her childhood was being reflected in the dream, and this is where we started as a way into the dream itself.

Following on from this point the next question to ask is: 'Do the feelings of this dream match up to those at other times in your life?' If the answer is yes, then jot down these other events and compare them with those shown in the dream. It could be that your dream is encouraging you to examine your current feelings about the past and offering an opportunity to bring them to God in prayer.

For example, a friend came to share part of a dream which he had when he was about to be ordained into the ministry. In his dream he was being interviewed by the man who would be his future vicar. He felt that he could not match up to the demands being made on him and that he would not have room to be himself. In the dream he felt conflict, and at first he wondered if this was God's guidance to him not to go to that parish. Further examination of these dream feelings revealed that they matched up to how he felt at times when relating to his father. The impending post of curate had awakened the tension he had when he tried to follow his chosen life and also get on with his father. Through prayer he was able to separate out his feelings and say yes to the vicar and go to work as his curate. It also gave him further opportunity to look at his feelings about his father and to work towards a more complete and accepting relationship with him. Both decisions have proved to be a blessing to all concerned.

Here then are a number of routes by which we can gauge the direction or basic thrust of the dream message. They may not explain the meaning of every symbol and element of the dream, but they help to pinpoint the 'punch-line' for which we are looking. Sometimes this is all that is needed to understand the dream. However, very often there is a need to press further in the dream and understand the messages contained in some specific symbol which may be critical for interpreting the dream. It is here that some difficulties occur, and we need to know what the symbols represent. I have therefore included some further guidelines on symbols in chapter 8.

A Resource for Spiritual Growth

As we open the door of our dreams to God we begin not only to get in touch with more of our lives, we can also give God access to this newly acquired awareness of ourselves. In this way we use our dreams, amongst other things, as a further resource for spiritual growth. It is interesting to note that the Septuagint (Greek Old Testament completed circa AD 70) translates the Hebrew word for 'interpretation', *peshar*, by the Greek word, *sunkrino*, which means 'to join together fitly'. It occurs, for example, in the Joseph stories in Genesis 40.8: 'They said to him, "We have had dreams, and there is no one to interpret them." And Joseph said to them, "Do not interpretations belong to God? Tell them to me, I pray you."' I do not think the application of this passage of Scripture is limited to just the dreams of the baker and the butler. It is saying that a true interpretation of a dream is in God's hands to give. Therefore it is no stretch of the Scripture to say that, by coming to a proper understanding of our dreams, we come into the place where God also can be and is working. Granted that this may not be a saving experience, as the fate of the baker indicates, but it is nonetheless an area where we should recognize the Lordship of Christ. To come to an interpretation of our dreams is to some extent to be ready and willing both to hear what God is saying to us and to offer what we learn back to God for his blessing.

Our interest in dreams and spirituality is increased when we make a further study of this word, *sunkrino*. It is not a common word in the New Testament, but it is used to describe how spiritual things are communicated by the Holy Spirit. Paul uses the term when writing to the Corinthian church: 'We impart this in words not taught by human wisdom but taught by the Spirit; interpreting spiritual truths to those who possess the Spirit' (1 Cor.2.13).[3]

The RSV marginal note adds, 'Interpreting spiritual truths in spiritual language'. So a link between interpreting dreams and spiritual reality seems established. There seems to be a parallel between working with the dream picture and unlocking the message contained within and the way that spiritual truths are learnt by those who are spiritually ·aware. Both are intended to facilitate personal growth and fulfilment. This is not to say that dreaming itself is a spiritual activity, but that, as we respond to our dreams in faith and with an openness to God, we give him further access to our inner lives and spirit. This is surely an opportunity to grow!

Unfortunately it has long been the practice for Western man to either ignore or depreciate his dreams. There is also the more recent question of using imagination in healing (as in the book entitled *The Seduction of Christianity*[4]), but surely one area which is clearly sanctioned by God for use in personal growth is that of dreams. And so, as we reown our dreams and seek to learn from them about ourselves and God, we do in fact open a door for growth which God has created and wishes to share in.

Now we shall examine in more detail just how dreams can be of use for our healing and wholeness, our deliverance and the deepening of our spiritual lives, our homes and our churches.

5 Praying with Dreams

Some years ago an elder of an independent church in Birkenhead asked if he could come round and share a problem he had. I knew Frank quite well; he was in his mid-fifties and was now living alone. His wife had died some years earlier, having come to a real faith in Jesus Christ shortly before her death. Frank was a Scot. The basic issue he wished to discuss was the fact that he found himself feeling increasingly reluctant to go home at New Year to spend a few days with his mother, who was a little distant from him by now. He had left home at the age of eighteen and had not lived in Scotland since then. His mother, now in her eighties, surely had not many more New Years to celebrate. She was not a Christian. What Frank wanted to know was whether his feelings indicated that the Lord was telling him it was not right for him to go north of the border. As we got into conversation he became increasingly agitated over his feelings. His reluctance began to change into a kind of fear which he could not explain. The fear was very real and, as he could find no apparent reason for these feelings, he began to cry.

'Why am I like this?' he asked. 'I don't hate my mother, it's just that we were never really that close. She had a lot of us kids to contend with and it was hard work for her.'

I asked him various questions about his relationship with his mother, and the only story that emerged was that life was hard and he was eager to get away from it all. His mother was now a small and frail person, and Frank couldn't remember being afraid of her although he had had his fair share of smacks when he did wrong, as did his brothers and sisters.

This was as far as we could go in counselling, but before we parted I asked him if he would mind if I laid hands on him and asked God to give him a gift of a dream which would unlock the door and take us further into his need. He was a little sceptical to say the least, but after I had explained some of the biblical insights on the value of dreams he agreed. He just sat in his chair and I laid hands on him and asked God to come to him when he was asleep and through the dream door give us a clue or a key to the source of his fear. A few days later Frank called around with his dream written down on paper. 'I never thought it would really happen,' he said. 'But the very first night I had this dream and when I woke up it was still there. So I immediately wrote it down and here it is.' Here is his dream:

> I was walking up the road to a house in Blantyre. [This is where he had lived as a young boy.] Outside the house I had to go in was a milk-van with the milkman scraping some dirt on to the back window. I wondered why he wanted to cover up his view. When I went into the house I was surprised to see a small boy sitting on the floor in the middle of something like flour which was scattered all over the floor. And now I am the boy and through the door comes a large, fearsome woman who is very angry. The woman grabbed the poker by the fire and hit the boy over the shoulder with it. Then I woke up.

I asked Frank how the little boy felt at the beginning of the dream and he replied, 'He feels uneasy, he knows he has done wrong and will be punished.' Next I asked him if he could get in touch with the feelings of the boy as he sees the large angry woman coming through the door. 'It feels exactly like I was feeling before, when we talked about how I really felt about going home to see mother. But I'm not afraid of my mother, am I?' 'It seems that you can identify with the boy,' I replied. 'Perhaps this is the time to take a step of faith and claim the boy of your dream as your own.'

So we turned to prayer and Frank simply asked God to help him accept the boy and the feelings attached, as these were obviously reflective of this actual feelings. It was quite an emotional moment and there were more tears and sobs and they were quite strong. Then Frank turned to me and said, 'That little boy is me, my mother did beat me like that once. I just didn't want to face it all again.'

It transpired that the dream related to an actual experience that had stayed with Frank and which he had tried to bury deep within him. I was able to point out to him that his feelings of fear were not that of a grown and rational adult, but the feelings of a little boy trapped and beaten by what fear described as a large and fearsome woman. Through prayer God had brought the buried moment to the surface within the dream. 'I must have been like that milkman,' said Frank, 'I just did not want a clear view of my feelings.'

Now that the truth was out in the open we again resorted to prayer, but this time Frank asked for forgiveness for not facing up to his fear and so choosing to drift away from his home and not have a proper relationship with his mother. I'm glad to say that he did go up to Scotland for the New Year celebrations and shared his experience with his mother and said that he was sorry. He later shared how this time with his mother released a sense of warmth between the two of them that had simply not been there for many years. Three months later, Frank's mother passed away. 'I'm so glad that God gave me that dream when he did,' he later said, 'We might never have got as close as we did.'

Praying for a dream to shed light on the situation provided an opportunity for healing and restoration between mother and son. Praying with the dream released the hurt feelings contained within and so brought the touch of God to an area that had, until then, been kept to himself.

There is, after all, a lot of scriptural precedent for this. When Daniel heard that the king was intending to slay all the wise men of the court, to which he and his companions belonged, because they were unable to understand the king's as yet undeclared dream, he prayed for understanding of the dream. His prayer was actually a request for mercy from a holy God, and God answered that prayer. The rest is a matter of history. On another occasion Daniel was given a vision about a coming world conflict. He immediately set himself to fasting and praying, this time not to understand the vision, but that he and his people might survive the coming battles (Dan. 10.1–3, 10–14). This praying into and around the vision was rewarded with his being shown more of the vision's implications: the people of Israel would survive, his prayers would be answered. This same connection between prayer and vision is illustrated in the book of the Revelation. John described himself as being 'in the Spirit' (Rev. 1.9) when he was called to see visions of what was to come. From time to time he felt the need for prayer for strength to stay in the place of the ongoing vision.[1]

In chapter 4, 'Opening the Dream Door' (p.32), I mentioned Ann who had recurring nightmares of being trapped in houses and followed by two men who leered at her. Here is the basic dream as it was before prayer:

> I am standing on the far side of a dark wood and I can see the house in the distance through the trees, but to get to the house I know I have to go through the dark wood. With me is a little girl holding my hand and she is very frightened. [Later discussion revealed that both adult and child represented the fear she felt as both as a little girl and now as a grown up.] I gritted my teeth and just ran through the wood pulling the little girl along with me. When I got to the house I went in by a glass conservatory and into the house itself. There was broken glass every-where and the locks on the outer and inner doors were broken. So I

could not be protected from the men who were coming after me. [It seemed that at this stage in the dream she was just the little girl.] I went around trying to shut the doors and windows but it was too late, the men were now in the house and they were leering at me and trying to frighten me. This is when I panic and try to run away but they always catch up with me. I feel so frightened just being in this house; I never feel safe.

Ann had had this dream on and off for many years and she nearly always woke up in a cold sweat. We decided first of all to talk through the dream along the guidelines suggested above, and it soon came to light that, as far back as the age of three, she was often left at her grandmother's house and this never felt safe. The real ordeal, however, was having to go to an outside toilet which to the mind of a three-year-old seemed to be down the end of a long dark path. It was always very cold down there and the journey back was even worse. She could see the lights of the house, but to get there she had to return up that same threatening path and her nanny never came with her. So she just gritted her teeth and ran back to the house. This fear had stayed with her from that time onwards.

Next we decided to pray into the dream picture and ask the Lord Jesus to touch and bring into the light the fears expressed, to break their stranglehold over Ann and to bring his love and healing to the inner hurts of the three-year-old child who was very much still a part of Ann's inner emotions. In other words we spoke into the dream story in faith. We gave the dream objectivity and treated it as live material within Ann's life. This was no 'faith-imagination' journey as such; because the material in question had actually happened, both in the dream and in experience before the dream, we had something fairly solid to work from. What was interesting and encouraging was what happened to the dream as a result of praying through the hurts it had reflected. Here is the dream she had after prayer:

In the dream this time I was just an adult. I was in the glass conservatory and I could see that the windows were broken and that there were no locks on the doors. But instead of being afraid I just thought, quite strongly actually, 'You need pulling down. You've had your day, it's time you went.' I felt really good to be able to say this. I had no fear and it was an exhilarating feeling. In fact I called in my friends and relatives and began pointing to all the things I used to be afraid of and tell them I wasn't afraid any more. I even called in those two uncles we talked about and said that I wasn't frightened of this house any more. I walked down to the toilet and said, 'Yes, and you will have to go as well.' There just wasn't any fear and it felt great.

This dream was in fact given on the night before we were due to meet again for counselling, when we had agreed to go further and confront any remaining fear. As she and her husband enthusiastically related the dream we all rejoiced, because we knew it was a real indication of what God was doing in her life and was about to do for her fear. Praying into the earlier dream had released the faith of the Lord into her life, and her dream reflected the result. In fact this second dream facilitated faith, through which we were able to explore further and come face to face with a spirit of fear which had attached itself to her life in those far off days of infantile terror. Together we commanded, in the name of Jesus, the fear to go, and because Ann had had that second dream she kept saying during this time, 'I know that the Lord has conquered fear and I shall go free.' And she was indeed set free; she actually felt the spirit of fear leave her body and, though tired, she knew she was free to get on with her life again. Now this faith to confront that from which she had always run was due to praying into a dream. By giving the dream space to speak its message and then to treat it as any other focus for prayer we can reach into it in faith and look to Jesus to touch any hurts or damaged feelings with his healing love. The dreaming which follows may well reflect where the path of faith will lead, as it did in Ann's experience.

It is worth while, just in passing, to point out that there are a number of recordings in the Bible where various people worshipped God upon hearing the message of dreams and then acted in faith according to the message they had received. Consider, for example, the encouragement a dream interpretation gave to a rather fearful leader called Gideon. In Judges 7.13–15 we read that when 'Gideon heard the telling of the dream and its interpretation, he worshipped; and he returned to the camp of Israel and said, "Arise, for the Lord has given the host of Midian into your hand."' The dream contained seeds of hope and he both prayed and acted upon it.[2]

Dreams and Meditation

So far then we have established that there is very real value in praying for a dream in order to facilitate further healing and that, by praying into the dream in much the same way as we would pray for other events, our faith is quickened and this is often reflected in a further dream.

'The heavens declare the glory of God; the skies proclaim the work of his hands. Day after day they pour forth speech; night after night they display knowledge' (Ps. 19.1–2, NIV). The Psalmist was able to gain insights into the nature and workings of God by meditating upon the creation itself. His imaginative and prayerful contemplation of the heavens led him to praise the living God. Similar times of meditation led to appreciation of God's care and commitment to mankind (Ps. 8.3–5); the need for forgiveness and cleansing (Ps. 24.1–5); God's steadfastness in the light of nature's calamities (Ps. 46.1–4f); God's security for the willing soul (Ps. 84.3–4). God's protection is like the city surrounded by mountains; his great knowledge extends to the secret moments of each baby as it grows within the mother's womb (Ps. 139.13–16).

Mention has already been made of the prophets of the Old Testament who gained insights into God's purposes by meditating upon some facet of nature which captured their imagination. Jeremiah watched an almond branch budding and through this, in prayer, understood that the season for God to act was about to come to fruition (Jer. 1.11–12). Amos was watching the harvest being gathered in, and from this God showed him that a swarm of locusts would come and devour the second crop about to be harvested (Amos 7.1–3). These pictures were used by God to provide a basis for sharing some word from the Lord. Meditation gave birth to prophetic insights.

Now there is no reason why dreams cannot be given the same opportunity for prayer and meditation. As far back as the Church Fathers there was the practice of sharing dreams in order to think upon them and gain prophetic insights. The *Didache* and the *Shepherd of Hermas*, both early-church documents which were widely known, described itinerant prophets who shared their dreams.[3] It seems that the early Church viewed dreams and meditation as parallel experiences; they gave access to the same source of reality – namely the spiritual. For someone like Tertullian, the soul is active even when the person is asleep and can often produce insights not yet grasped by the dreamer.[4] Gregory of Nyssa takes this issue of meditation a step further when he writes: 'When asleep the senses and the reason rest and the less rational parts of the soul appear to take over. Reason is not however, extinquished, but smoulders like a fire, heaped with chaff, and then breaks forth with insights.'[5] This means that we can make our dreams a gift to God over which we can pray and ask the Lord to give us greater sensitivity to ourselves and more awareness of where we are in our spiritual journey. As I have said in my earlier book,[6] very often our reply to the question which God asks, 'Where are You?' (Gen. 3.9), can be, 'Here is a dream which has touched me deeply, help me to know myself better as you guide me through it.' Just meditating upon a dream and relating it to this one question can often help us to find out not only where the dream places us in our outlook but also how our faith in God can relate to this. Consider the following dream for example:

> I was on a train, and in the carriage with me were seven other 'figures'. Six of the seven figures became aggressive and I felt very threatened. One of the figures started twisting my arm up my back but I wouldn't yield and, after a while, he left me alone. The train then stopped at a station and the six figures started fighting amongst themselves, and in the mêlée they fell out of the carriage and on to the platform. As the train started again and the doors had closed, they realized that they couldn't get back on to the train although they ran alongside as the train was moving. I was left in the carriage with the other person. I should explain that the 'figures' were real people and not shadow images.

Prayerfully going back through the dream, basing all observations on the 'Where are you?' approach, produced the following responses. The six fighting figures in the train fitted in to a number of pressures that were troubling the dreamer, ranging from business to domestic issues, all of which he knew he was wrestling with. This observation then led to a prayer of calling upon the Lord to help him sort out the pressures. Repeating the question in connection with the train journey simply underlined the fact that he was journeying through life and, although it also carried these figures, life would still go on. This brought some comfort. Again the question was asked of the silent but observing figure in the dream. This indicated that the Lord was aboard his journey and although he wouldn't make any decisions for the dreamer, neither would he leave him to fight without support. When the question was addressed to the one twisting his arm the answer was that this was that part of him which was trying to twist how he saw himself. He said that he suffered from that well-known evangelical disease which is called 'Dislike yourself'. The man twisting his arm was trying to distort his view of himself in the light of the problems he carried. Interestingly enough, in the dream, he wouldn't give in to this. This encouraged his faith because it registered the fact that he was getting stronger in his self-acceptance. Despite his problems he was not going to fall into the old trap of saying that these problems were there because he was somehow unacceptable to God or himself and he was being punished. Finally, asking the 'Where are you?' question to the six figures fighting among themselves as the train pulled away produced the response that the journey will go on and

Christ will still be aboard. The fact that the figures were fighting among themselves underlined that the pressures he was going through in his life were inter-connected to some degree.

Following on from these basic insights the dreamer then prayed about the problems individually and repented of any bitterness he had had towards God because of his difficulties. Later he wrote in a letter, 'Whilst I still have these problems, I am trusting the Lord to work them out, and I believe that my attitude is now positive instead of negative. Things have recently become better in respect of my job and this has been a great encouragement.' So by meditating upon the dream and just picking up any observations or insights which occurred he was able to deepen his spiritual insights into how he was reacting to his situation and then hand this over to God in prayer. This benefited him immediately. It also provided him with some specific objectives for prayer, and his perception of how he understood the role of Jesus in his life was sharpened. He had been bitter because God had not stepped in and sorted things out for him. His dream told him that God was with him, but that he would have to make his own choices and live with himself and his faith as a consequence. He began no longer to expect God to shelter him from facing up to things nor to cushion him from reality. Instead, God would go through the trial of faith with him.

So, meditating upon a dream is to rehearse the dream before God, picking up and taking hold of the feelings that arise. By giving these feelings a voice and offering them to God, we gain some perspective to our faith-walk at that time and in that circumstance. There may well be reflections of our childhood that we have not really touched upon properly.

I well remember sharing some counsel with a friend who dreamed of times in her childhood when she felt happy, but in reality her parents were either too ill or too occupied to share her childhood with her. Hence her dream though happy was tinged with a feeling of absenteeism. As she meditated on the dream picture she turned and offered her childhood times to the Lord Jesus and thanked him for the gift of those days. As she did this she believed that God renewed in her life the awareness of his love for her, and it felt good to know that God celebrated her childhood too. The teaching of Jesus in Matthew's Gospel that not one sparrow falls to the ground without his notice, suddenly became quite a powerful indication of how God had been and still was a good heavenly Father to her. From that day on she began to feel a more complete person, and this in itself opened the door for further ministry which resulted in a healing of long-standing back trouble plus the diffusion of a lot of aggression towards her parents. You see, with her mind she completely understood her parents' incapacities but her feelings, which came up from that of the lonely child, grew resentful of their absence. The dream reflected the childhood feelings which had not up to then been given a proper voice in her life. So coming to the dream in an attitude of prayerful observation helped to shed light on a part of her life which she had been denying to herself and, consequently, to her God

Many of our dreams contain a full range of feelings which we may have been repressing as we have gone through life. It is our way of coping. I have met a lot of people from both a strict Evangelical or Catholic background where the voicing of problems or hurts has been regarded as a failure of faith. In the desire to express the belief that we are indeed a new creation in Jesus Christ and that 'the old has gone and the new has come' (2 Cor. 5.17), they have tended to drift into the error of 'empty triumphalism'. By this I mean that we have indeed the new life of Christ within us by the presence of the Holy Spirit, but this does not mean that we have eradicated the problems of our particular humanity.

Many Christians would readily agree that we need God's continuous forgiveness of our sins, but they baulk at the idea that we continually need God's healing touch upon the consequences of our sins within our lives. That is the healing of our hurt or damaged past which is often reflected in our present feelings. Our dreams will provide one of the ways in which God can help us to get in touch with these feelings that we have blocked out of our waking lives. Therefore, to pray into or meditate upon our dreams is one resource among many for potential spiritual growth.

Dreams and 'Fantasy Journeys'

As a conclusion to this section on dreams and prayer I want to make short reference to the subject of 'fantasy journeys' in counselling. This refers to a scripted exercise where the individual is encouraged to sit comfortably and listen to another read out a short journey which the other is encouraged to imagine himself making. It could consist of walking along a familiar country road and imagining meeting Jesus as your faith and biblical understanding portray him. The journey would continue with Jesus sharing some special encouragement or guidance with you before your return on the journey to where you began. People would then be encouraged to share this with each other in the group if they so wished, the object of the exercise being perhaps to underline or locate how you perceive your walk with God at the moment and what it means to you. Another fantasy journey is about meeting a wise old man by a fire who gives you a special gift which you are asked to become, in order to appreciate the spirit or intention with which the gift was given. The range is quite wide and varied, and they can all help us from time to time to tune in to how we are reacting to certain issues of faith and life.

Now the dream is not exactly a fantasy journey because it is a personal document which we have written and we must be careful not to tamper or distort the message it contains. However, having said this, the dream can be used in a parallel way to a fantasy journey. This is often useful if the dreamer wishes to appreciate his own dream more fully through the help of another. The dream can be recited and the helper can build in at certain points some logical extensions to the dream but which develop from out of the dream itself rather than being the total invention of the helper. For example, as part of the work Frank and I shared as mentioned at the beginning of this chapter, I asked him to retell the dream a second time, now more slowly than before. When he came to the point of just entering the house in which he was to find the small boy I asked him to pause and said, 'Now as you stand at the threshold of the house, just take a little time to have a closer inspection of the room. Is there anything in particular you see that you wish to mention?'

He paused for a little while. (Incidentally, he was sitting comfortably in an armchair with his eyes closed, purely for the sake of concentration.) Then he began to say, 'It is quite a dark room but I can see that the wallpaper is a heavy pattern that looks rather triangular in shape.'

'Anything else you want to mention?' I asked.

'Over in the corner I can see two sets of iron bunks. Man, they're huge!'

It was at this stage in the dream recall that Frank began to say that the whole picture was that of a house he could just remember living in during the earlier years of his childhood. This was of course the clue to the fact that his dream was more than likely bringing to the fore an actual moment in his life. In fact this was as far as we got in this approach to the dream, when he said that the dream was about something that had happened to him but that he didn't want to face up to it before.

Other extensions to the dream could be to ask the person if they see anything else in the dream picture from a different perspective. For example, one lady had dreamt of being in a wide open plain with nothing to see except a shrouded figure approaching her from afar and which was slowly coming closer. As she related the dream a second time I asked her, before looking off into the distance at the approaching figure, to look down at her feet and to tell me what she saw, if anything. Her reply was that she couldn't see her feet at all, try as she might. But somehow she knew the ground around her was hard and unyielding. Then I asked her if she could turn around and see if the dream would extend to what was behind her. Her reaction was very interesting, she said that she knew she couldn't look behind because there was nothing there, and that this know-ledge frightened her. The fear related to the fact that she could not see her feet, and she said that both pictures gave the same feeling of being tied down so that she couldn't move. This was as far as we felt we should go then in this direction, and so we continued with the flow of the dream.

I must point out that, in this exercise, the aim is to stay with the basic dream but to look a bit deeper and see if there is relevant material which had not been acknowledged. This particular person was able later to see for herself that the dream was about a time when she was on the operating table awaiting further treatment which she knew would be quite painful. The work had to be done, she was trapped. This also helped to clarify why she could not see her feet or look behind. When concentrating only upon the approaching figure, she failed to pick up other relevant material.

Another possible approach could be to ask the dreamer at some poignant part of the dream to share that moment with Jesus in a verbalized prayer; this often helps deepen faith, as it is an immediate response to the dream message. Or the person could be asked if she wants to call on someone else to come and share in the dream and then to reflect on what that has done for her, if anything. Once that has been done, she can be encouraged to ask that person to 'leave the dream' as it were, so that the rest of the dream can be recounted normally. This time the helper can check out how she feels as she moves on in the dream, and how this contrasts with how she felt when she first shared the dream with you. These are just some suggestions of how the dream can be employed as a parallel 'fantasy journey', only I believe it is more productive than the latter because we are dealing with the individual's personal script. So let me encourage you to come to your dreams, when the need arises, in an attitude of prayer and openness to God and so provide yourself with another resource for spiritual and personal growth. It is, after all, just a stepping stone from here to incorporating dreams as an element in the process of healing to which Jesus has called all people.

6 Healing with Dreams

In this chapter we shall cast our net as wide as possible so as to include a full range of healing needs for which dreams can be employed. This includes physical and emotional healing, deliverance ministry and bereavement counselling. The apostle Paul, I am sure, was forever grateful that a relatively unknown Christian called Ananias acted upon his vision. For in this vision he was plainly told about Paul's Damascus road encounter and that, through his prayers, this opponent of the Christian church would be both healed and commissioned by God. What far-reaching implications this obedience to a dream had for the spread of the Christian gospel! It is my contention that, whenever we respond sensitively to our dreams, we take a step of growth in our lives. If for nothing else, this is because we are learning to stay in touch with every part of our lives. For the Christian of course such insights are naturally shared with God for his blessing and guidance. So, in a general sense, offering the dream to God is a form of healing.

Forgiveness

Some years ago when we were living in Whalley Range in Manchester, I was asked if I would meet and talk with an 18-year-old man who was quite disturbed. Martin had become a Christian some years before and had been progressing quite well in his faith until the age of eighteen. His mother had died of cancer some years before, and her faith had sustained her to the very end. Martin's father had been a clergyman but was now in care, having suffered a nervous breakdown some years before his wife's death. Apparently, Martin had been getting drunk on a number of occasions, the police had been sent for and he had been taken into custody until he 'dried out'. When we first met he was distant and not very happy to be talking to me. However, we established a mutual trust and friendship which exists to this day. As he shared more of his story he began to tell me of a dream he kept having; even when he was awake this picture would break through into his mind:

I was sitting around the table for Sunday lunch. We had just come back from church. My dad is standing at the head of the table in the process of carving up the roast. Then suddenly he begins to shout and he starts to attack us with the knife. My mother manages to get out of the way but my sister is wounded before she gets away. Then there is only me left and Dad is making a funny noise and begins to chase me. This is as far as the dream picture goes.

It transpired that every time this picture, and the events it linked in with, began to surface in Martin, he ran away for shelter. The only shelter he could find was to get so drunk that he would not remember anything at all. His neighbours had told other people that when he was drunk they could hear him shouting out and making other incoherent noises as he broke things in the house. It seems that he was acting out the violence he felt from his father. His father had indeed had a nervous breakdown and had exhibited threatening and sometimes violent behaviour within the home. What had wounded Martin so deeply was that his natural need was to receive love and affirmation from his father but all he felt he received was antagonism and distancing.

After coming to the place where this cycle of behaviour was established, I suggested that it was time to put the dream, and the fear it contained, to rest at the foot of the cross. I explained that perhaps the best thing to do was to go back through the dream picture, but this time within the context of committing all that we were about to do into the hands of the Lord Jesus. This he agreed to do although he felt a little apprehensive at the time. And so Martin began to unfold the dream picture as he sat calmly in an armchair with me beside him. He rather expected, I believe, to be overcome with the power of it all and shrink at its violence. This was not to be. What he discovered was that, thanks to the grace of God, the picture the dream revealed of his father, was a broken and confused man and not a threatening tyrant. He had been unable to be objective because of the fear and hurt he had carried inside himself for so many years. He had wanted to love his father but he felt that his father was dangerous to be near, and this caused him great frustration and anger. Now he could see with some clarity into his past and begin to feel things in perspective about his father's behaviour. But this in itself was not enough to help. We can have all the knowledge but it will not of itself bring healing or release. There is the need for a step of faith. It was at this point that I suggested to Martin that he bring the father he saw in his dream to the place of forgiveness at the cross of Christ. Now that he saw the issues with more clarity he agreed to this. His short prayer was quite moving; it was something like this:

> Dad, I have found it hard to accept what had happened to you and to Mum. I think I blamed you for some of what Mum went through. But I see that you were suffering too and so, Father, I forgive you for you did not know what you were doing.

A direct consequence of this act of forgiveness was that the destructive cycle of drunkenness began to be broken in his life. Further sharing produced repentance on his part for his actions, and this included going to some members of his family whose property he had damaged. They were equally forgiving and helpful to him, both then and for the future.

Forgiveness will always bring release and renewal to a person's life. Forgiving others, and so receiving forgiveness for our sins from God, is an integral element in the prayer of our Lord Jesus Christ (e.g. Matt. 6. 12). To forgive another is to be in the place of receiving forgiveness and the cleansing of our lives (1 John 1. 9). This place of forgiveness is also the proper basis for the healing prayers so often required in our lives (James 5. 16). If then this ministry is so beneficial to our lives and to those whom we forgive, then it is only right that we employ the same in relation to the hurts and needs reflected in our dreams.

I think of the dream of a lady who had only recently discovered that her husband had been having an affair with another woman. Together they had worked hard to restore their marriage and had been for counselling together. The dream, which occurred a number of times, showed her coming up behind her husband and burying a hatchet in his back! When asked if she had indeed 'buried the hatchet' with her husband, she was honest enough to admit that she knew she still held some resentment against him and wasn't sure if she could or wanted to trust him again. The implications of this dream were obvious; there was still room for forgiveness and trust on her part. I'm glad to say that this did indeed take place.

So use your dreams to check out how you see your standing with others; it could be that there is a need to forgive or indeed repent of your attitude. It may be that you have been holding on to hurts you have received from those close to you and it is time to bring them to God for healing and release. Mind you, let me also caution you to be sensitive about how you do your forgiving! Do not be like the Christian in the fable who went up to another person in church one day after hearing a sermon on forgiveness and say, 'I just want to say that I have asked the Lord for forgiveness as I have hated you all these years and I thought I should tell you.' If the other person does not know of your feelings then offer them and that person to God in repentance and forgiveness. The release which God gives is just as real. However, if your dream touches upon something which both parties involved know about, then perhaps this is the time to take a step of faith and first bring the issues and the people in the dream before God in forgiveness and then go and extend that response to the people themselves. I often find that this ministry of forgiveness, or letting go of something held against a person, has particular usefulness for those who are bereaved of the very ones they need to forgive.

Bereavement

Some months ago I was speaking at a dinner, and after sharing some thoughts on emotional healing, I closed with some prayers. I became aware that there was someone present in the meeting who had a problem concerning their mother who had recently died. So as part of my prayers I encouraged whoever it was to let go of their hurt feelings towards their mother and learn to forgive, even though their mother had died. Afterwards a man came up to me and said that this part of my prayer had challenged him deeply and that he knew his need to forgive. In fact he went on to say that his bitter feelings coloured the whole of his relationships and even prevented him from getting more involved in his church life.

> I always have this picture of my Mum on her death bed [he said]. She looks so weak and frail, not at all like the strong-willed person I found it so hard to get on with. I was sorry she was dying of course. At the same time I wanted to talk about how she had hurt me, but I daren't. Now she is dead, and I feel that I am stuck with these feelings.

The picture was both a memory and a frequent element of his dreams. He wanted to know how to get into the act of forgiving, as his Protestantism made him feel uneasy about going any further. So I encouraged him to join me in prayer and to use his dream/memory as a basis for this. I explained to him that although his mother had died and, as far as her ultimate salvation was concerned, this would be unaffected by our prayers, nonetheless there was a very real place for him to let go and even say goodbye. He gave himself a little moment to focus in to the actual death scene of his mother which he had relived time and again in his sleep. Then he began to say that he had been hurt by her and that he had often felt angry and he wanted to be angry then, but it would not really help. He forgave her for her neglect of him and he himself apologized for his own reactions to this and asked the Lord for help and forgiveness. The next moment was perhaps the most moving, in that he simply said goodbye to her and with this farewell came his grief and tears, things which he had denied both to himself and his mother. Afterwards he told me that he felt immediate relief and a sense of renewal and freedom. He had been storing his bereavement feelings inside himself, not sharing them with anyone, not even his God. This had led to his feeling drained and tired and increasingly frustrated with his life.

However, bereavement can also be a healing experience, as it helps us to express our sense of loss and pain and so begin the journey of coming to terms with our human frailty and limitations. Even our God and Father has entered into this arena of loss when his son Jesus Christ entered into death upon the cross. He will therefore walk with us as we go through a time of loss ourselves.

What had been the turning point for this man was that the dream/ memory, once he had focused upon it in prayer, released so sharply his immediate feelings and the underlying feelings of love for his mother which he had not dared own as his own. It was the progression of expressing his hurt feelings, followed by an act of forgiveness and confession, that enabled him to get underneath to the starved feelings of love which he had not allowed to be voiced before.

So the dream picture helps us to focus on where the hurt feelings are located, and this can be for some the turning point from merely knowing something must be done to actually doing it!

Some people also dream about their deceased relatives at a time when they have actually come to terms with their bereavement, and so the dream picture can often be a pleasant one, as explained in chapter 3. What I would encourage the dreamer to do is to consolidate that time of 'letting go' by speaking into their own dream picture and saying goodbye to the individuals concerned. They can give themselves room to share their feelings of positive warmth as they have now come to the moment in their lives when they are able to carry on because they have come to terms with the experience. This can be a most valuable exercise for us, as in this modern world many people are not themselves present at the death of a close relative or friend and they often feel cheated of a valuable moment in their lives. By utilizing our dreams in this way we can deal effectively with our need to say goodbye and so journey on through the feelings of bereavement itself.

Emotional Healing

All dreams deal with the way we really see our world of experience. I have already pointed out that this means capturing feelings which we may not have admitted properly to ourselves when awake. Bearing this in mind, it becomes clear that dreams can be a very useful resource for clarifying some of our feelings and then bringing them into the orbit of the healing touch of Jesus Christ. Our dreams provide us with a home-made indication of how we are reacting to various things. It may often appear to be different from what we have said in our waking life. For example, Ann Faraday, in her book *Dream Power*, mentions a time when her husband was about to conclude with a colleague a business deal involving a lot of his own personal capital. A few days before completion of the contract her husband dreamed he was going to a celebratory meal with his prospective partner. It included salad and as her husband dug deep into the salad bowl he found, to his disgust, that underneath there were many different insects crawling about. What could this dream mean? (Having a wife who specialized in dreams was an obvious advantage.) As far as he knew the deal was sound and he was happy with his prospective partner. He admitted to one or two gut feelings of indecision but nothing more. He disliked insects and they made him feel uncomfortable. So he decided to check out his dream feelings sensitively, and by this he meant he employed another person to check out the business deal; it was found to be fraudulent! Needless to say, the contract never went through. He had not properly monitored his 'gut' feelings, but his dream had been more faithful. It showed to him that underneath the immediate feelings of celebration there were things that had made him feel uncomfortable.

There is then a discernment quality to some of our dreams, and by giving them proper attention we can learn more about ourselves than perhaps we are properly admitting. This need to know ourselves before God is never more true than when it comes to our need for emotional healing. So dreams can be an invaluable help in facilitating such healing of our inner lives. Now there are a number of ways in which we can approach a dream in order to discover all the feelings they contain and so bring ourselves to a place of faith where we can respond to our true and complete feelings so that we may be healed.

One of these methods is known as *Gestalt*. This is a German term for 'whole' and refers to that moment of healing when we are able to bring more of our inner lives and choices into harmony with the whole of our lives. The term was used by Fritz Perls in his particular approach to counselling. He would encourage people to let the different elements of their problems 'speak'. For example if a person was sharing a relationship say with a parent, Perls suggested that the individual place an empty chair by them and speak directly to the parent as if they were sitting in that chair. Then they would be encouraged to swap chairs and assume the role of the parent as they felt him or her to be within their experience. The 'parent' would then be encouraged to verbalize a response to the first statements made. The purpose of this exercise was to clarify to the individual how they really saw themselves in relationship to that other person and how that other person had influenced, and might still influence or shape their lives. Once discovered, a choice could then be made to change and go forward with a more complete control of the future.

Perls would extend this exchange of roles as far as inanimate objects as well. The following is an example of how he would treat a dream. First the basic dream story:

> I was driving along a smooth road in a nice car. It was pouring with rain but I was able to see where I was going although it was difficult.

What Perls would do first was to ask the man in the dream how he felt in the dream driving the car. The reply would be something like, 'I feel in control and making the decisions of where I am going despite the weather. I am nice and dry inside this car.' Next he would encourage the dreamer to give a voice to the car itself so that it might say how it felt. The response would be something like, 'I am the one who has the power. Without me, the driver cannot go anywhere. I don't like this weather as it makes me feel wet and miserable.' Then the road itself would be asked to respond similarly: 'I'm fed up with people driving all over me. Nobody takes notice of me and I don't like this at all. Get off me!' Finally the rain would be given a voice: 'I can spoil all your plans or at least make things very difficult for you. If I like I can spoil your vision so that you will have to slow down.'

Treating a dream in this manner releases the dreamer's perspective from a number of angles. The punch-line of the dream is that the driver is making a journey through life, but closer inspection reveals that he is not as completely happy about how things are going as he may indicate. By listening to the voices of his dream characters and symbols he gives himself permission to listen to all his responses and, by bringing them together in the best kind of cohesion possible, he enters a 'gestalt'. Incidentally this method also helps us to discover the meaning of many of our dream symbols which may at first puzzle us. For Christians, this approach to dreams can be a method of surrendering to the Lord all that we discover about ourselves which may be new and which therefore needs to be consecrated in prayer.

I am reminded of Jesus' words concerning the exercise of faith and prayer, 'You can say to this mountain, "Move from here to there," and it will move. Nothing will be impossible for you' (Matt. 17. 20 NIV). Here Jesus is encouraging his disciples to be direct with areas that need confronting in prayer and even to speak to them in order to have them moved. Now this is a good word for guiding us in employing this *gestalt* method in our dream work. In the name and authority of Jesus we can speak to our personal mountains of pain and confusion, and tell them to be removed.

The way in which this kind of healing of emotions comes about is that we also need to locate just where the 'mountain' in our lives is, and how and where we want to relate to it in the future. Gestalt work with dreams is one good way among others.

The following is an example of how this method can be employed. This dream work took place before approximately 45 students who were on an Introduction to Pastoral Counselling course. This was live work and not fabricated counselling.[1] The dreamer is Elizabeth who is also one of the course tutors and the wife of an Anglican minister; the counsellor is Di, a Christian much involved in a counselling and healing ministry.

ELIZABETH: I am by a forest of English trees. There are mature oaks and silver birch. They are well established trees. I am standing on a well worn, red-packed earth pathway. The forest is friendly, I know it well. There is a house, it is red brick and has two stories. It is still being built and has no roof yet. There are no windows or doors and there is a packed earth floor. Upstairs is a kitchen sink. I'm feeling a little nervous with having people around. But I'm inquisitive about the dream. I'm cautious, there may be a surprise around the corner. The last time I came to the house I saw the sink. It is against the left-hand wall which is red brick. There is a floor and yet there isn't a floor.

DI: What do you say to the sink?

ELIZABETH: You are in a strange place here. You belong in a utility room, not upstairs with the bathroom. You have a drainage hole but no grid to stop things going down.

DI: Become the sink.

ELIZABETH: I'm very solid and thick, and heavy. I'm white china inside and out. I've got a few chips in me. I'm an old sink. I like being open to the sky, I'm glad there is no roof. Thank you [house] for giving me a place to be that is up and not downstairs. I can be quite useful to you. I'm big, we fit in well together.

DI: Become the house.

ELIZABETH: I'm feeling a bit weepy because I am alone in this forest. People come and go and visit me, but I'm still alone, incomplete. I'm incomplete and not much use. The builders left a long time ago. I don't want to be here any more. He left me incomplete, lost interest in me. I feel disowned, abandoned; just another project. Come and finish me and make a good job of me (*voice getting a little stronger here*).

DI: Is he hearing you?

ELIZABETH: He's nowhere around. I'll move on to a housing estate. The only thing I can think of is to invite others to build around me. I can't dismantle myself. Part of me wants to stay in the forest. (*Pause ...*) I want to be the person looking at the house. But I'll stay with the brick house. I feel stuck! I want to go and I want to stay. I want the best of both worlds. I'm going to have to – I don't want to – to get up and go. My practical part says, 'Do something,' and my feeling part says, 'Stay!'
                 (*When talking about the feeling part, Elizabeth touched her throat and the back of her head and neck*).
                 The feeling part wants to be in the trees and forest, in contact but not bothered by them. It knows I'll be lonely here and the winter will come and the people won't ... (*voice trails off*).

DI: Is this a question for the brick house to decide?

ELIZABETH: (*Tears at this point*) I don't want to be stuck. I want to be 'that' person.

DI: What does the brick house want?

ELIZABETH: I want a roof, leaded diamond windows, plastic guttering, tiles, a water barrel, a glass front door, proper flues, carpets and an open staircase. I want each room carpeted. I don't want a garden; I want the forest. I want to be a house where people can come, rest, retreat and go again. To be able to shut your door and say, 'I want to be empty now.' I want to ask people who come to build these things into me. I see a child with a brass knocker and she wants to put it on the door.
                 (*Speaking to the girl*) Thank you. Let's put it on a wooden

	board outside. I'll put it at a height where you can reach it.
DI:	How does the little girl feel?
ELIZABETH:	Pleased (*smiles*). Knockers are usually out of her reach. I let her in the house.
DI:	How does the house feel now?
ELIZABETH:	I'm complete except for the roof. I need to ask some strong men to bring a beam and roof struts.
DI:	Ask them.
ELIZABETH:	(*Struggling with this*) It's some of the men folk in our church. (*Speaking to the men*) Peter! James and Gordon! Please will you help me (*tears now flowing*).
DI:	What's happening?
ELIZABETH:	(*Still to the men*) I want you to help build me up.
DI:	Are they hearing you?
ELIZABETH:	Yes. (*Men now speaking*) We would love to help, we love you, care for you and want to help. (*Tears now stop*) They are working together.
DI:	How are you feeling now?
ELIZABETH:	I feel very honoured.
DI:	Are you receiving then?
ELIZABETH:	(*Relaxing*) I'm thinking of the second part of a hymn, 'Give me grace, that I may receive.' (*Pauses here.*) Grant me grace that I might let you be my servant too!
DI:	What's happening?
ELIZABETH:	I've got to get the tiles on.
DI:	How?
ELIZABETH:	(*sighs*) I've got to ask people for help.
DI:	(*Long silence.*) What's happening now?
ELIZABETH:	I've got to ask the ladies, Ruth, Jenny, Sally, Susan, Emma and Jean. I feel very incomplete as I think of them and see their faces. There is a sort of nakedness; I'm there and exposed. I want to say, 'Come and clothe me.'
DI:	Pick one to speak to, which one?
ELIZABETH:	Emma. 'Emma I see you watching me and looking at me and I feel naked and incomplete and I want you to come and clothe me (*shows a concerned look*). I want you to understand me, I know that I have needs too.'
DI:	Is she hearing you?
ELIZABETH:	Yes.
DI:	What is she saying?
ELIZABETH:	(*Emma speaking*) 'I always thought you were so strong and capable and didn't need my help.' (*Replying to Emma*) I put on a front (like the door). I want you to pray with me. (*Tears here.*)
DI:	Say this again to Emma.

ELIZABETH:	Be aware of my needs.
DI:	Again.
ELIZABETH:	Be aware of my needs.
DI:	Again.
ELIZABETH:	Be aware of my needs.
DI:	Say it again and really make her hear you.
ELIZABETH:	Be aware of my needs, minister to my needs Emma (*voice getting more determined*); because I need you. (*Speaking to Di*) Emma is surprised (*sighs*). I feel relieved, I've got through to her at last.
DI:	What does Emma say?
ELIZABETH:	She says, 'You're such a stupid woman, I have just as many needs.' (*Speaking to Emma*) You're older, Emma, and a wise person; don't compare yourself with me. I need you. (*To Di*) I think that's good!
DI:	Are you aware of your roof now?
ELIZABETH:	Yes, it's half on now.
DI:	What do you need to get the other half of the roof on?
ELIZABETH:	I need to talk to Susan. (*Pauses here.*)
DI:	What's happening?
ELIZABETH:	She's a delightful person, a bit scatterbrained. Don't be scared of me, Sue, don't be shy – I'm human. I don't want to talk shop, about support groups. I enjoy your sense of fun and freedom, of light-heartedness. The way you can put a feather on heavy objects.
DI:	Make your demands of her.
ELIZABETH:	(*Sighs*) It feels difficult to get through to you, Sue. I want you to be a buddy, a laughing friend; let me have fun with you.
DI:	Make your demands of her.
ELIZABETH:	Tell me what you're afraid of, don't put me on a pedestal.
DI:	Tell her what you '*do*' want.
ELIZABETH:	(*Sighs*) I find you hard work, Sue, I reach out and reach out (*extends hands and arms in front*)
DI:	Notice how you didn't make a positive demand.
ELIZABETH:	I realize I'm scared of you Sue; you know how I feel. You sit and smile smugly.
DI:	Choose what you want to do now.
ELIZABETH:	I want to be open with you, Sue. And I want you to tell me when you feel frazzled.
DI:	Is she hearing you?
ELIZABETH:	Yes.
DI:	What is she saying?
ELIZABETH:	(*nods*) She gives me a giggly laugh. She is saying, 'O.K. I will.'
DI:	Do you believe her?
ELIZABETH:	Yes, it will take time.
DI:	Have you been aware of your roof?

ELIZABETH: Yes, it's 90 per cent complete.

DI: What about the 10 per cent?

ELIZABETH: Ooh! I need to talk to Jean.

(*Talking to Jean*) Stop making me your mother! Stop giving me your silly hugs: I don't like them, you're trying to get round me.

(*to Di*) She hears me.

DI: If you are not her mother, tell her who you are.

ELIZABETH: (*sighs*) She wears so many hats in church; she's around the house so many times. She tells me so many stories about her family.

(*To Jean*) Don't steal counselling over a cup of coffee. I don't want to know about your family problems.

(*To Di*), I want to say to her 'F.O.'

(*To Jean*) Stop draining me!

DI: Tell her what you *do* want.

ELIZABETH: I don't want you to come in the house. Go in David's study. Stay out of my home and don't come unless I invite you. I don't like you peeping around the door.

(*Louder*) Get out of my space!

(*To Di*) I'm scared of hurting her feelings. I can say it here but not to her.

(*Sighs*) Jean you work very hard for the parish.

DI: Tell her straight.

ELIZABETH: (*Very determined*) Jean get off and keep off my patch!

DI: Repeat this.

ELIZABETH: (*Sighs and says to Di*) You're too persistent.

(*At this point Elizabeth felt stroppy and rebellious.*)

DI: What is happening?

ELIZABETH: (*Props herself up on her knees.*) I'm afraid of hurting her.

(*To Jean*) Jean, I feel the tension of wanting to speak straight to you but I'm struggling with the fear of hurting you. I relate to you much better if you respect my space.

DI: Then demand it.

ELIZABETH: (*Elizabeth repeats the above.*)

DI: Louder!

ELIZABETH: (*Sighs.*)

(*To Di*) Don't be so persistent Di. Jean is so persistent. I fee I struggle with Jean. I'm always pushing her back, always saying no, always being nice.

(*To Jean*) Always avoiding you. You drain me, you're damn persistent.

DI: What do you want to say?

ELIZABETH: I'm bargaining.

DI: Make your choice.

ELIZABETH: I want my space.

DI: Then demand it of Jean now.

ELIZABETH: (*Pauses, emphatic breathing.*) I want you to understand, Jean that you are not to come into my home unless I invite you.

DI: Was that clear enough?
ELIZABETH: Hmm, yes.
DI: What is she saying?
ELIZABETH: (*Pause.*) She looks hurt, taken aback; but she has heard me and I know she'll respect that.
DI: Look at the roof now.
ELIZABETH: (*Pauses and thinks.*)
DI: How is it?
ELIZABETH: Complete. Windows? Yes. Door? Yes. Floor? Yes, there are wooden planks. Sink? Yes. Waste pipe?
             (*Pause, sigh.*) It's still not connected. That's where all the rubbish goes down.
DI: What do you do now?
ELIZABETH: Get more pipe and things. I've done that now.
DI: Look in the sink, at the outlet.
ELIZABETH: There is a new, shiny, stainless steel grid. The chips have gone. There are flowers in the sink.
DI: Carpets?
ELIZABETH: Hmm! (*Meaning OK*).
DI: Stairs?
ELIZABETH: Hmm!
DI: Going to the door?
ELIZABETH: Hmm!
DI: People around?
ELIZABETH: Hmm!
DI: What do you feel about the people?
ELIZABETH: They're excited and pleased about the house.
             (*They say*) 'Hey! Let's go visit!'
             (*Elizabeth speaking now*) The door is glass. It is strong and unbreakable and it opens inward. Just now it is a summer's day and so it is open. I'm on the inside and I say to the people, 'I'm shut now, come another day.'
             (*To Di*) It feels good.
DI: Make it personal.
ELIZABETH: I feel good, I feel roomy and spacey and comfy.
DI: Is there anything you need to say to the house before leaving?
ELIZABETH: (*To the house*) You're a pretty good sort. I like you. You're completed now, better than the way I imagined. You've got a roof now; I'll be better now for when the winter comes.
DI: How are you feeling?
ELIZABETH: Sad. It's just because I'm leaving the house, I think.
DI: You don't have to leave your house. You can take it with you. You can shut the door whenever you need to.
ELIZABETH: (*Pauses and nods with a smile*) I'm thinking of the song, 'Come and go with me to my father's house.'

Here the dream work ended after a session of one hour and three minutes. It was followed by a time of prayer and committing to the

Lord for his healing all the relevant insights and feelings that had come into the open. This is not the place to analyse the dream for the benefit of the reader, but I think that the issues concerning the dreamer were fairly clear. We can see how the imagery of the house and the visitors, coupled with the *gestalt* approach, helped the current feelings which were contained within the dream symbols to be sharpened and owned.

Once this has been done the next step is to surrender the new ground gained to the Lord and then trust him for an opportunity, where practical, to put any new resolutions and discoveries into practice. This is the beginning of emotional healing. We begin to see things that we had repressed or blocked from our lives but which took their toll upon us. And, however minimal the things our dreams reveal for us, to offer them in trust to God is to allow him into what has been, so far, forbidden territory to both us and our Lord. And is this not a freeing experience? Thank God, it is. This then can also be a constructive way of dealing with the fears buried within our nightmares.

We have already seen that nightmares have to do with the 'unfinished business' of our lives at the moment. It is unfinished because we are unable or unwilling to face up to some major upset within our lives at that point. However, our dream life is faithful enough to present us with the relevant material so that the need for healing or help is at least signalled to us. In working with others in a counselling ministry I am always pleased when people share their nightmares, because I believe that it is a direct, although sometimes painful, route to the inner hurt. So nightmares are messages of strong colour. Consider the nightmare which Pilate's wife had and the effect of it. She said that she had suffered much in a dream on account of Jesus. We can only guess what this was all about but it at least reflects a deep inner conflict which she was having concerning Jesus. Her note to her husband was sufficient to cause him to become uncertain about how to deal with the crowd's hunger to kill Jesus and to release Barabbas and wash his hands of the whole affair. This was unlike the normal behaviour of the Pilate of history who was a ruthless and stubborn character. It seems that his wife's nightmare affected him. More than this we cannot say.

It is generally agreed that nightmares originate from two basic sources: those derived from objective experiences, usually from childhood but not exclusively; and those derived from fear of our own impulses. Consider for example the following dream:

A young woman dreamt of her now dead fiancé turning up in a ghost form in her dreams. He scathed her for her sexual attraction to another man. He would point his finger at her and make her feel really upset. But before his apparition came to her she would wake up in a disturbed manner.

The young woman's boy-friend had died some years earlier in a tragic accident and she was only now beginning to resume her life. Another man had come into her life, yet part of her was feeling that she was betraying her former boy-friend and that she shouldn't be enjoying her new relationship. So she began having the nightmares described above. In working with her she was encouraged to speak out to the ghost in her dream and to share, in a positive manner, how she wanted now to live her life. Although a little reluctant at first, she was able to say to her former boy-friend that it was time for her to get on and live a normal, healthy life. She was not going to blackmail herself with guilt, as there could be no going back to the past. So with some determination in her voice she told her ghost to leave her alone. And that was the end of dreaming this nightmare. As an afterthought she realized the significance of the ghost in her dreams: it was not so much a figment of fear but a realization that her feelings for her former boy-friend were dying and that they were not as strong as she had consciously thought they were. And so this confronting of the nightmare gave her strength to free herself of some guilt and fear that had still been within her.

Some nightmares reflect actual moments which have been repressed deep within. The nightmare may be the only indication we consciously have of there being some inner trauma which still needs attention. Consider the following example of nightmare from Arthur Janov's book, *The Primal Scream*:

> I was being attacked and something had me backed into the corner of my room. I tried to escape and ran to my neighbour's house, where I planned to call the police for help. I kept dialling the wrong number, and I just couldn't get the police.[2]

This dream had persisted for some time and despite repeated telling of the dream always ended with the frustrated telephone call. During a further time of sharing the nightmare Janov interjected the account by calling to the dreamer to 'dial the right number!' She yelled back that she couldn't remember it [although the number is as well known as 999 is to us in Britain]. However, with a little persistence she finally managed to dial the right number and out came a horrifying scream. She screamed for ten minutes, writhing and thrashing on the floor.

A little later it transpired that as a young girl she had never received help from her parents and so she felt rejected whilst at the same time had to do everything for them. The dark thing in her dream was a representation of how she felt, that the future, like the past, looked dark and hopeless. She had grown up without hope and needed to get free, and her nightmare reflected her depression. The difficulty of not remembering the phone number was significant; it represented her childhood fear that she might not get the help she needed in life and this would dash her fleeting hopes once and for all. So she chose not to know the phone number of the police. The nightmare was about her childhood experience of rejection and once out in the open she was able to assume full responsibility for her own life and to enter into a fuller enjoyment of living.

Any nightmare, sensitively explored, will inevitably lead to one of these roots. Once this is arrived at, the work of healing and deliverance can take place. It is like uncovering something that has lain close to the surface, which, now it has been properly listened to, calls for a response of faith.

I have already mentioned the lady who had the recurring nightmare of being approached by a hooded figure (see page 30–1). Here is some more detail of that dream :

> The cloaked figure is coming closer and closer towards me. I cannot see the lower half of the body and its face is all but covered up. The figure is covered in a deep red and its arms are stretched out in front of it as if it wants to greet me. I feel a great deal of fear and want to get away, but I can't and so I begin to panic. Before things get any worse I notice that the figure is disappointed at my reaction and then I wake up.

Together we worked back through the nightmare point by point. The basic message was that there was some threatening fear here. We needed to know its root so that, in the name of Jesus, we could bring it all under the authority of God. When I asked Jan, the dreamer, to look closely at the figure and tell me if there were any other details she noticed she remarked on the really bright redness of the garment. 'It's funny,' she said, 'red is a colour I really like, but I'm not comfortable with it in this dream.'

So again I asked her to inspect the redness because it didn't seem to correspond with just the colour red. She found this difficult to do at first. Then I encouraged her to speak to the redness and to ask,

'Who or what are you?' This took a little time and then she said, 'It's blood.'

'Whose blood is it then?'

After some more pause for thought she said, 'It is my blood.'

'How do you feel, seeing your blood on someone else?'

'I want it back, it's mine. I don't like my blood being there, it's part of me.'

'So what are you going to do about that?'

Here she invited the Lord Jesus to help her confront the masked figure.

'In the name of Jesus, I demand my blood; it is not your's, it is mine. I also demand that you go back from me and take off your mask.'

It was at this point that Jan stopped doing further dream work. She said that she now knew what it was all about, but that she had at one level been unwilling to face up to it all. When she had given birth to her daughter, she had been badly stitched by the surgeon and had been left in considerable pain in the delivery unit. She had to wait there for almost an hour until another surgeon came, undid the stitches and repaired the damage done through negligence. She was very angry but also felt helpless lying on the table. The second surgeon had done his best but Jan had felt quite devastated by the experience. However, she had never been a person to demand her own rights and this was true of her upbringing as well. And so, locked inside her, was both the anger and the fear of that moment some six years earlier. By working with the dream she was able to voice some of the anger and confront the fear. She later went on to say that it was quite significant in her nightmare that she could never see the lower half of the masked figure, and this matched up with the view she would have had that day as she was lying down and could only see horizontally. Incidentally, when we later checked out how she knew that the figure was disappointed despite being covered up, she said that the second surgeon was trying to make up for the damage done earlier and so was a helper, but she was just too afraid and upset to appreciate his remarks.

The immediate benefits of working with the nightmare was that the very real fears within it were exposed for what they were and this in itself was a release. It was also a relief to know the nature of the fear because this now meant that we could make a proper and particular prayer response. We could have gone on praying about a general fear and got nowhere. The Bible tells us that perfect love casts out fear (1 John 4.18), and the way this works in practice is to surrender the now identified fear to the Lord Jesus. If there is a need of repentance and forgiveness, this can be included at the beginning of the prayer. In Jan's case she simply owned up to her own feelings of helplessness and anger at that time in hospital and entrusted them to the Lord for his healing. We then invited the Lord to build into these moments of fear the presence of his accepting love so that the 'power' of that fear be broken and Jan herself freed from any ill effects of those times. Our prayer time was completed with a lovely sense of the Lord's peace and his inner assurance that he had done a work of inner healing.

Let me just end this account by saying that the memory would always be there in some form, but that it would no longer have any power over her and hence the nightmare had no cause to return. So however upsetting a nightmare is for the individual, it also offers a clue to a need for healing. Besides this, it is our own 'signal of distress' which we ignore to our peril.

Deliverance

Moving on from nightmares I would like to share just a few thoughts about deliverance and how dreams can sometimes be a useful indication for the need for this ministry. This is not the place to explain fully the reasons for this ministry or detail the ways in which it is effected. Suffice it to say that it is a much needed aspect of healing and, with the developing interest in the occult, it is more than likely to be needed still more. However, discernment is the necessary process we have to negotiate before we come to the conclusion that the problem to be confronted is one of spiritual warfare. Dreams can be of some help here.

Very often when people have approached me for counselling and possible deliverance from spiritual bondage they say, amongst other things, that they have been having strange dreams which have been frightening them. These have a different feel from those nightmares and recurring dreams which reflect some unresolved tension in a person's life. They usually take the form of the dreamer being attacked by a very definite evil presence or manifestation. Such dreams also tend to spill over into waking life, so that very often it is hard to distinguish between a dream or an actual event. The effect is to drain the person of any ability to resist or defend themselves. There is also the inability to rest from the problem at hand. This time there is no bailing out of the dream before the awful crisis occurs. The dreamer usually tastes the full effect of the dream picture. It is this characteristic which I see as a major clue that we are dealing, not with a nightmare, but with some sustained spiritual attack or manifestation.

A number of the people with whom I have worked have reported that after attending a spiritualist healing or clairvoyance meeting they have begun to have disturbed sleep. Some time ago I received a phone-call from a person requesting deliverance ministry, and I went to see her. Sitting beside her husband she told me that over thirty years earlier she had had a curse put on her by a medium with whom they had been sharing a house at the time. She and her husband had been quite active in the movement themselves and they still retained an interest in things 'occultic'. They personally did not attend a church nor were they practising Christians. During the discussion she told me that since the time of the curse and her involvement in the spiritualist movement, she had been having recurring nightmares in which a shape in her bedroom would lie on top of her and almost suffocate her. She would wake up feeling breathless to find nothing there but a very real sense of fear. Since these dreams began, she had become increasingly agoraphobic and hardly went out of the house.

After saying a little about the Christian principles of having nothing to do with things clearly forbidden to us in the Bible,[3] and that this included spiritualism, I suggested to her that we take seriously the indication from her dreams that she was under demonic attack and that, in order to combat them, we would focus on the shape in her dreams. She agreed, and so I first attempted to lead her in a prayer of repentance and forgiveness for involvement in the occult. She did not want to do this, and so I explained the dangers of deliverance without commitment to Jesus Christ (Matt. 12. 43–5). Then I rebuked the curse upon her in the name of Jesus and simply addressed 'the spirit of the dream' in the name of Jesus, bound it and commanded it to go from her from that moment on. There was no apparent manifestation of deliverance apart from a great deal of crying on the woman's part.

A few weeks later I returned to see her and her husband. The woman reported that after my first visit, she went out of the house and walked to a local library, visited one or two people on her way home and felt perfectly calm. These were things she had not been able to do for some years. Also a long-standing problem with her feet had now been healed. Most interesting of all was the fact that she no longer had those dreams or feelings of a presence in the house. I then repeated the counsel about renouncing anything to do with spiritualism and to repent of her life-style which had excluded the Lordship of Jesus Christ. She said she would consider this and was happy for a local Christian minister to start visiting the home. What was interesting was that, through our recognition of the dream shape as a genuine spiritual attack, God was able to bring a measure of deliverance.

So if you are finding that you have certain recurring dreams which reflect a direct spiritual attack upon you and those close to you, then take time to check up on your spiritual journey. Have you had any dealings with spiritist activities or perhaps engaged in what you might have considered to be some harmless pastime such as reading tarot cards or having your palm read or reading your horoscope? It could be that you have unwittingly opened up your imagination and spirit to a spiritual enemy, and, if this is so, you will need to seek help and healing.

This kind of dreaming reflects at the very least a disturbed spirit, be it the dreamer's or be it demonic. Whichever it is, it should be treated quite objectively in a deliverance prayer. Counsel should also be offered regarding repentance and renunciation of all things occultic. Without this there is no real letting go by the individual of their involvement in such things.

Some years ago I spoke on the subject of 'Jesus the Wonderful Counsellor' at a large house-church in the Manchester area. Afterwards I prayed with a lot of people who came to share various needs; it was a very privileged time in my experience of ministry. Of the people who came forward, there was a man called Sean who wanted me to pray for his wife's healing. The more we talked and shared, the more it became apparent that it was Sean who really needed the most help. Later he told me how he would have this recurring dream which really upset him: he would see his mother (now deceased) come and stand behind him and then place her hand on his head and say something to the effect that he now had the power. The dream then showed that he was in the power of some evil spirits who would now control his life. Indeed, he had had prayer for deliverance on a number of occasions but with no success. So I simply prayed in the name of Jesus that the evil spirits revealed in his dream be bound and cast out of his life. One by one came manifestations of the evil spirits in his life. In fact at one stage he said, in a slightly altered voice, that the spirit of violence was about to be revealed. Needless to say I called on the name of Jesus, that he forbid any unnecessary show from the demonic realm, and there wasn't any. A little while later he said that he felt a real measure of freedom within and that his marriage was vastly improved; however, he still felt as if there was a hand resting lightly upon his head.

It was at this point I tackled him about the rest of his dream picture, the person of his mother. He told me that his mother had been a medium and that he had completely disagreed with her beliefs – so why was he still in some kind of spiritual bondage? I asked him to tell me what his mother was doing in the dream and he said it looked as if she was saying goodbye. So I asked him to share with me how in fact his mother had died and whether he was there at the time. He said that he was there and, just before his mother died, she raised her hand and laid it on Sean's head, and said, 'I give you my blessing.' The next step seemed quite clear to me, I suggested that he needed to turn to his mother, using the dream picture, and to say whatever he wanted in the way of declaring his love for her, but that he needed to renounce her blessing as it came on the basis of her mediumship. What followed was a very traumatic experience for Sean, but he did just that and, although he was very sick at the time, he also gained his full release as a child of God. Incidentally, his love for his mother is just as real and strong as it ever was; he just repented of and renounced receiving her spiritualistic blessing. He and his wife and family have gone on to enjoy their lives together with much more freedom than they have had for many years.

So, in conclusion, I simply want to say that if your dreams do reflect spiritual and demonic attack, then take stock of your spiritual life, see if you have been trespassing into things which God has forbidden to you. It could also be a reflection of spiritual damage which has come down through the family background, and you may need to check this out carefully before proceeding further. Once again, examine the feelings of the dream and, if they match up with those of a person under spiritual attack, then yes, there is the need for deliverance prayer. It is wiser not to attempt this on your own, so do seek the guidance of your minister or one who is able to help in this area.

7 Dreams for the People

In this chapter we shall consider some of the ways in which dreams can be shared for their value in the growth and healing of various groups and communities. Most of our dreams will be concerned, not with just our lives, but also with those who are important to us – like our family and friends, or the people we work with or worship with. Occasionally we may have a dream which is of importance for our community and so needs to be shared at that level in some way. This was certainly true of men like Martin Luther King Jnr. Upon his return from receiving the Nobel Peace Prize, he had a dream of what could happen in America if all the communities would work for equality and acceptance. The dream took the form of walking up to a mountain top and being able to look out and see how the world might appear to God. The imagery of the dream was more than likely suggested by the passage in the book of Deuteronomy where Moses went to the top of the Mount and could see over the valley to the Promised Land. King shared his dream in a number of large rallies which he later addressed, and many influential statesmen have testified to the eloquent power of the dream which has motivated them into a more active work for racial harmony.

We may not rise to such heights in our dream sharing, but it will be more than surprising if our dreams do not have something to say to those near and dear to us.

The Family

The sharing of dreams in a family often helps to draw that family closer together. Sometimes it is very difficult for children to share with adults their own fears as they may not get a sympathetic hearing. I well remember being asked if I would come and pray with a girl in one family because she was having horrible nightmares of being attacked by a furry monster. Her parents had done their best to reassure her that there was no monster there and that it was just a dream. Frankly, this approach doesn't help. It merely confirms in the child's mind that we do not think her fear is real as well as being a way of saying that her dreams are unimportant. Rather than ask the girl to talk directly about her fear I asked her to share with me her dream, it was quite simple really:

> When I am asleep, I wake up in my dream. At the bottom of my bed I can see the head of a very furry animal and it climbs up on my bed and comes near me. I know that it is not safe and I tell it to go away, but it won't and so I cry.

I asked her why it was not safe, she said that Mummy had told her it was very dangerous to let animals get on the bed. I discovered that this was a reference to the girl's mother having scolded her for having her pet cat come and lie on the bed with her at night. The scolding had instilled feelings of fear and danger, and her dream reflected back these impressions. So I encouraged the girl to reach out to the animal in her dream and to stroke it, if she felt that would be all right. She found no difficulty in responding to the dream in this way and indeed thought it was a nice game. The moment she reached out to the animal it began to purr, and she saw it change from a frightening animal into her pet cat. 'I'm not frightened of her now,' she said. From that time on the nightmares ceased.

Now what I want to underline with this example is that we can reach into our children's fear in a non-threatening way by using the resource of dream when possible. The girl thought it was a game but, like all games in life, there is a process in learning bound up with it all. Children usually remember their dreams better than adults and are quite happy to talk about them and learn from them. In our family, as I began to collect dreams and work with them, my own children wanted to come and share their dreams with me. In fact we started our own family dream diary. Here are two dreams amongst others that my daughter Emma had when she was about seven years old; she told the dreams to my wife, Carole, who wrote them down:

> I was in the library and my shoes kept changing shape. There was a boy on the banisters of the stairs and he was making them change. My Daddy left me and went off on the bike. I didn't like the dream very much.

> I am with Dr Who and he is moving about a lot in his police box, and he leaves me alone on the pavement. I started to cry. I feel the same way as before when Daddy went off on his bike.

By her own deduction Emma knew that these two dreams had something in common. It had to do with the feeling of seeing me going away on a bike. So I asked her how she felt standing there on the pavement. She said, 'You are always going away and I feel that you would rather do that than be with us.' She was referring to the fact that at that time in my life I was travelling quite extensively around the country preaching and counselling. I would only be home perhaps one night a week, which meant that I was virtually absent for the times of putting them to bed. I was also out fairly early in the morning and so did not see much of the family then either.

Emma's dream message conveyed so much unshared emotion and feeling that I was simply convicted of my life-style as far as my involvement in the family was concerned. Her dream voiced the fear that she could never bring herself to speak about otherwise, namely that I was more interested and in love with being away than being at home with her. It was a fear that she had no idea of how to voice, and then there was always the worry that if she did talk about it she might find her fear to be true, and this was an unacceptable risk for her.

Although I will not say that I have solved the problem of staying at home sufficiently, it was this dream encounter with my daughter which made me really want to try. I had always known that I should change my routine of going away but I had not really been motivated enough. But the dream message came with such impact that 'I was moved' to listen again and try to change. And so I thanked Emma for her dream and said that I was sorry and would try to be a better father in future. Today I am truly grateful for her love and life and the way we just enjoy being with each other.

Sharing dreams in the family, then, offers a low-profile opportunity, especially for the young, for touching some of the fears and hopes which we find so hard to talk about directly. By making children aware of the importance of their dreams at an early age, they will grow up with the idea that dreams are not just things that happen to them, but their own internal vision which they act out in sleep in order to tell themselves something of importance. By encouraging children to think of their dreams in a positive way like this, we provide them, from an early age, with an easier and more natural access to their inner life. It also helps them to be more aware and accepting of all that they feel and think.

Dreaming is also good for parents!

I dreamed that a man phoned up to ask if we definitely wanted to send the children to Meadow Lane Infant School. I said, 'Yes,' and put the phone down. Then I had all the following worries: how was I going to get them there in the morning without the car? It meant uprooting them again for a few months; Emma had had good reading books at the other school; what was I going to tell the other school?

This was a dream my wife Carole had, and she also provided herself with the interpretation at the time of writing it down. 'I think this dream had something to do with my not realizing I hadn't got the car for the following morning and that I have now got to transfer my lay-reader's course back to Manchester. I was Emma in the dream.'

First some background explanations to the dream. At the time we were about to leave Nottingham where I had been in training for ordination and move to Greater Manchester where I was going to take up the post of curate. This would mean that both our children would have attended three different primary schools in twelve months. Meadow Lane school was in fact the one that our children were about to leave. Parallel to this, Carole had applied for training as a lay-reader when we had previously lived in Manchester, but had been told by the Bishop to wait until we moved to Nottingham and then to reapply. At Nottingham she had been told to wait until we moved back to Manchester diocese and then reapply! Needless to say she was feeling messed around by the church authorities. The basic feeling reflected in the dream also touched upon the fact that Carole had not had a particularly happy family life as a child. With our children being moved around so much, this had made her feel as if she was treating them as she herself had been treated, and she knew how miserable that had made her. So there was guilt at the thought of giving the children an unhappy time plus her own frustrations at being mistreated over her desire to be trained as a lay-reader.

As she shared the dream we were able to clarify more sharply some of the factors at work in the way she related to both our children and the need not to be over-protective of them. It also helped us all to appreciate our role within the family and how we too had been responding to each other. The result was a releasing in our family relationships which helped us all to appreciate each other more. I think our home was a more whole place to be as a result of this dream time.

A few years ago I received a letter through the post from a lady who lived in north Lancashire. Her dream had to do with moving houses, and the central part of the dream concerned the feelings aroused as the family (according to the dream) stepped into the hall of their new home. It was dark there, and this disturbed the family and made them wonder if the house itself was wrong for them. A little while later I agreed to meet with the lady and her husband to discuss the dream more fully. As we talked together about the dream the husband also registered the fact that they wondered if they had done the right thing in moving house; had they been disobedient and as a consequence were they under spiritual attack? As we reworked our way through the dream I asked the wife who was with her as she entered the hall in her dream. She said, 'All the family, that is except for our other daughter.'

It turned out that they had a teenage daughter who was mentally handicapped and living in a home where she received constant care. By moving to the new house they were not as easily able to visit their daughter. This had brought a little tension to the mother, but the father was honest enough to share that he had not easily got on with this daughter and was beginning to see that he had perhaps been rejecting her because of his difficulty in relating with her. He had felt somewhat happier at moving away, as this decreased confrontation with his own feelings towards his daughter. However, he now felt that perhaps he should ask the Lord to help him really feel love towards his handicapped daughter, and so together we prayed for release and healing within his feelings. I later heard that a subsequent visit to see his daughter had been much more fruitful than usual, that the father was beginning to feel a real love for both of his children and that this had led to a step further in spiritual renewal in his life. The sharing of the dream helped to pinpoint the feelings of tension within the family over the move to the new house and so pave the way for ministry and healing.

So the sharing of dreams within a family can be a useful resource with which to focus on some areas which we may have found difficult to touch upon. It is not threatening either, because before any real sharing can be done the individual concerned chooses to share the dream. There is also a 'fun' element in working with dreams, especially for children, and this helps reduce some of the tensions that tend to block meaningful sharing. However, with any sharing of dreams within the home we should always caution each one to have a humble spirit and to offer the dream with a readiness for everyone present to say what they feel is there and to compare this with the thoughts of the dreamer. Consider, for example, the spirit in which Joseph shared his dreams with his brothers! Hardly a cause for celebration at the time. His brothers knew that their father had made Joseph his favourite son and concluded that Joseph had been fantasizing about his future status: he had become a braggart. The result was almost a foregone conclusion. So there is a time to share a dream and a time not to.

The Fellowship

There is no doubt in the opinion of the general public, that the Church has been losing its influence and authority within the community. This is only partially due to the theological indecision and confusion which has characterized the churches' leadership. It is also because the Church has failed to be an agent of healing for the whole person. Of all public institutions, it should be the Church of Jesus Christ which offers practical help to people seeking better understanding of themselves and their problems. Unfortunately it was the Church which not only heralded the general mistrust of dreams within the Western world; it also frowned on the sharing of feelings, as they were considered less reliable than faith. This latter point may be true for doctrinal issues and a Christian's standing before God, but feelings do indicate where and what a person is living through at certain times in their lives. Therefore, dreams in particular are a valuable resource through which people can learn about themselves and grow into the wholeness of life for which God created them.

Some months ago I had a call from a leader of an evangelistic organization who asked if he and some fellow workers could come over to the vicarage and share in a 'dream-workshop'. He had heard that I had been giving some teaching on dreams to members of one of their mission teams and conducting some group work on dreams afterwards. And so it was that we shared together in two sessions, each lasting about two hours. A little while later I heard that for one or two who had been present it had been a turning point in their understanding and appreciation of dreams. In our work together we had discussed how to share dreams in fellowship groups and then to pray about the messages that emerged from each one's dream. Apparently it had even helped to improve the working relationships of some of the staff and bring about a better spirit of fellowship. Praise the Lord!

As we know, the fellowship we enjoy as Christians is improved the more as we learn to share, truthfully and in love, the things seen.

This is as true of blessings as it is of difficulties. Naturally we need to exercise common sense about what we do share. All sharing is an invitation to the other to come and touch, in Christ's name, a part of ourselves, and this is a vulnerable place to be. After all, we might be rejected or misunderstood. Yet sharing a dream is a very helpful way to let the fellowship around you appreciate what is happening inside your life and to see how you are feeling. So often, I feel, our fellowship in church is merely cerebral. We share thoughts and insights, comments and views, but very rarely our inner life and feelings. Working with dreams is to open the door for the other to come inside. So it must be done with prayer and sensitivity.

In the original group of youth workers and evangelists I was working with, we spent some time together sharing our dreams. (As I was pastoral adviser to the team, we had already established a certain level of openness and trust.) Each person was to talk out their dream, first as they had written it down and then again but in the first person throughout. This was to help the dreamer to publicly own the dream there and then rather than to treat it as something that had happened and was finished with as far as the group was concerned. Each one had complete choice as to which dream they brought. Also, everyone was able to ask questions and offer reflections (rather than deductions) on the dream. The following is one of the dreams which was shared:

> I am in the vicarage, in the room where meetings are held, where we've been working (the team that is). I am finishing off some work, the rest of the team have gone home (I don't mind, I'd rather it was finished). It looks like we've been making toilet-roll dolls. I'm finishing those off, putting faces on them. There are one or two other things too. It's 6.30 p.m. but at least I've finished and I'm ready to go home. I'm pleased to go, the rest of the team are returning, they tell me to get a move on or I'll be late for youth club. I try to explain that I've only just finished (I want to go home first). But they won't listen (I'm angry). I am running out of the vicarage and getting my car door open. Russ is saying that I should go in and get things sorted out.

It seemed natural to pursue the dream picture further to see where it might lead. What came out was that the dreamer felt calm once out in the car park talking to me because she knew she could choose to say 'No' and not come back inside; she felt in control. However, once we started to try and get in touch with the feelings reflected during the scene previously, inside the vicarage, the feelings switched to disturbance and a little panic. After some sharing and comments from the group, the dreamer said that she never really felt listened to by the group. There were also some comments about how she felt that the leadership of the group was not definite enough; she felt that to some degree she was left, like others, just to get on with things and that this was not appreciated enough or recognized enough. The final comment related to how there wasn't enough real sharing being modelled in the group.

Now although these comments may sound critical, they actually helped other members of the group to see themselves through the eyes of another, and this helped the fellowship to become more alive and supportive. There were no recriminations, because the group knew they were being allowed to see and hear how one of their number felt. They were able to touch part of her story and, although it didn't solve all the problems, it did help to focus for the whole group, one of its prime needs. So fellowship was improved. From the moment this sharing was done, the rest of the group had a much clearer grasp of how to pray for God's blessing upon their work and personal growth.

I have always been struck by those questioning words to Gehazi of Elisha (who himself would have been an Old Testament equivalent of an established charismatic), 'Can't you see, she is in bitter distress?' (2 Kings 4. 27 TEV). Here was a woman who was pouring out what seemed like invective upon the prophet, and his servant could see only embarrassment and bad behaviour. But Elisha knew there was some deeper reason and was honest enough to admit that until then the Lord had not shown him what was the problem.

This is quite often the reason why our fellowship fails to grow; our relationships deal only with things on the surface, and we never allow others real access to our human spirit. Well, this sharing of dreams, however minimal the issues, does indeed open the door inwards and we begin 'to see' what is there. After all, it was in a similar context to this that the prophets shared their dreams and visions with their disciples. They received the visions and even recorded them for our benefit. And so we must not make the mistake of rejecting dreams out of hand, but learn to listen to one another because here too we may begin to hear the voice of God for the group.

Just to complete this section on sharing dreams, there is no reason why dream-sharing cannot be extended to larger groups, such as churches. There may well be hidden perspectives and feelings about the life of the church which the leaders need to hear. Home groups and prayer groups could be encouraged from time to time to give room for working with dreams. This would ensure that anybody who wanted to explore some of their own feelings would be given a hearing. There may well be the sharing of feelings regarding the vicar or pastor: which church doesn't have its share of critics? Working with dreams would provide an opportunity to talk such things over with a bit more space than an actual confrontation would provide. It gives room to be more open about why we feel things and so offers a chance to be more objective about ourselves. There may still be the need eventually to go and share with the person concerned, but having done a little work beforehand we should be able to bring to such moments more maturity and therefore more healing.

Sometimes we teach and preach about great themes such as forgiveness and renewal in our churches but find little response. Sharing dreams may help a person appreciate their need to forgive or be helped in a more challenging and motivating way. When I was at the ACTS '86 conference in Birmingham in July 1986 I was asked if I would just listen for a few minutes to a couple of dreams. We were all about to rush into another of the excellent John Wimber healing seminars and so we had not much time. I had never met the person before and so I prayed for guidance as I concentrated upon the dreams being shared. Without going into much detail the main dream message pictured this person trying trying fly a rocket from out of his living room but the tail-piece was stuck on the floor. In the dream his wife was standing by but was apprehensive about the whole affair. I believed that the dream was about a conflict of wills in the person's life, that he was ready to take off into some form of Christian ministry but had not yet really talked and shared it with his wife, because although she would stand by him it would not be in a really supportive way. So, trusting to the Lord's guidance, I shared this and recommended that before he did step out into any form of new work he really talk about his fears and feelings with his wife so that they would at least be together in whatever they decided to do. I must also say that I am not usually as direct and abrupt as this in working with dreams. However, my new-found friend was quite overcome to hear this and he gave me a really nice hug. He said that he knew that what I had said was true; he just needed to hear it through another. And so as we parted to go into the seminar he assured me that he and his wife had some praying and restoring of their relationship to do. It is interesting to know that he knew what to do, but he had not 'heard it' in such a way as he needed to. I certainly talked about the need for forgiveness, but linking it in to the dream message earthed the exhortation into the reality in which he then lived.

So too for our prayer groups, folk who dream of relationships where there is breakdown or hardship can then be encouraged to apply the steps of forgiveness which they heard in the sermon but which may have sounded just a bit too much like theory.

To conclude this section on sharing dreams in groups, we can see that this offers a gateway for growth in self-understanding and a chance to improve the quality of life in family, fellowship and community. There is so much disintegration within our modern society, and this is coupled with a deluge of therapies which seemingly offer self-improvement but without belonging within a committed and caring environment. The Christian is part of the family of God, both in church and in his own home – how much more therefore should we be providing a genuine opportunity for growth but which will be growth within a loving fellowship of faith? Amongst other things, dream work offers just such a ministry of growth and belonging.

Prophecy

Before concluding this chapter I want to say a little about the prophetic cutting edge of dreams and visions. It has already been pointed out that one of the indicators of spiritual renewal is that mature men will continually dream dreams:

> This is what was spoken by the prophet Joel: And in the last days ... I will pour out my Spirit upon all flesh, and your sons and your daughters shall prophesy, and your young men shall see visions and your old men shall dream dreams. (Acts 2.16–17)

The whole context of the original word in Joel's day was that of God restoring the knowledge of his presence amongst his people. It was to be a time of renewal among the faithful and, as a result of this, everyone would be able to receive the benefits of the Holy Spirit. What had been limited to the prophets and spiritual warriors and leaders in the Old Testament days was now being shared with all men and women without discrimination.

Now we have seen that dreams and visions conveyed the prophetic word of knowledge to the people of God. This same function is still available as a resource for healing and guidance. There is no reason why God cannot present us with his prophetic word for our lives or for our churches and fellowships.

The New Zealand evangelist, Bill Subritzky, tells of a time when he was preaching in the islands of Vanuatu (formerly New Hebrides) and had a vision of a great spiritual power called 'Division', which he believed was behind a lot of the unrest in the islands at that time; there were indeed two political factions seeking to take control of the government at this time. Bishop Derek Rawcliffe (now the Bishop of Glasgow) arranged for Bill to meet the then Prime Minister of the islands. This man proceeded to share a dream which had haunted him for some time and which his clerical friends had been unable to interpret. Bill found that he already had the interpretation, as his own visionary experience had indeed prepared him for this moment. The Prime Minister's response was to endorse Bill's ministry the following day as he officially opened the Anglican Synod, and this certainly paved the way for a movement of spiritual renewal in the islands the outcome of which was to bring real peace among the political factions. The fears of a coming revolution were thus put to rest.[1] Here is a very striking example of the prophetic cutting edge channelled through a dream.

This 'word of knowledge' function of dream can also be used on a more parochial level in order to bring God's healing and help to others. Consider the following dream account from Dr Ken McAll:

> Once, in the half-awake, half-dreaming world of the early morning, I had an image of a friend called Mabel whom we had not seen for eight years. In the 'dream' she was yelling out of the third floor window of a strange brick building. This meant nothing to me at the time but I scribbled the name Mabel on a piece of paper and forgot about it.
>
> That same evening, as I was driving home from work, I was held up at a traffic light. As my frustration and impatience grew I felt the Lord was directing me to turn left. I argued, 'No, I want to go straight home.' 'Turn left,' he commanded. I was alone so ... I turned left, feeling rather foolish. I nevertheless drove very slowly so as not to miss anything. Then from the right-hand side of the road a woman's voice shouted, 'Doctor Ken! Doctor Ken!' I glanced up. Our friend Mabel was leaning out of an identical third-floor window of my 'half-dream' of that morning ... Mabel explained (eventually) that early that morning she had come to this block of flats to collect her sister because they had just heard that their elder brother, who had lung cancer, was dying. The sisters had spent the day trying to contact me. This incident proved to me that one of the most important aspects of early morning listening to God is the fostering of an attitude of continual listening throughout the day.[2]

Dr McAll is saying here that listening to God is available through the experience of dream as well. This would have sounded perfectly natural to the Old Testament prophets.

As we carry our concerns, loves and likes for family and friends upon our hearts and often into our dreams, it should be no surprise that the Lord may choose this means to give us an insight as to their needs or his will for them. I had an experience of this nature back in 1967 when I was the leader of a Christian Union in a large Polytechnic in Birkenhead. My dream pictured the fellowship all seated in an attitude of prayer and fellowship. However, they all seemed oblivious to the fact that snakes were secretly coming amongst them and entwining themselves around their chairs. In the dream I felt the Lord say that one of the girls in particular was in great danger as well as the fellowship being under threat of disunity. I shared this dream with a friend. We prayed together about it and we both felt that the dream was referring to a particular person who had recently joined the fellowship. He was slightly older than the rest and exuded a spirit of zeal and understanding. However, after the dream, some of us noticed that he seemed to be quietly going around charming people to join his own private fellowship group. When we tried to talk to him in private he began to shout and say that we were only jealous of his superior spirit and with that he left the fellowship taking some people with him. It later came out that he had seduced the very girl who was pictured in the dream, this despite tactfully trying to caution her about getting too involved. It was a salutary experience for me and taught me at an early stage to be objective but balanced about such experiences of revelation in dreams. The dream had at least prepared us for what was to come, and I am glad to say that the majority of folk who left that fellowship, after a period of disillusionment, did eventually return.

Prophetic insights arising from dreams may be compared with the spiritual gifts mentioned in 1 Corinthians 12 and Romans 12. These insights are evidence of the spirit of renewal at work within the Church, and as such there should be room to evaluate their usefulness and to see if indeed the application of the dream has proven to be for the 'common good'. This is after all the same test that is given to the charismatic gifts.

8 Getting on with Dreams

> The dream is an invaluable counsellor. We cannot pray for a better one. It is with us every night, charges no fees, and makes no demands except that we listen to it and learn to detect God's voice in symbolic language. The dream seeks to co-operate with His great purpose; to help us to realise every part of our potential and to bring us into harmony with ourselves, God and the world around us. There is no better way to get to the heart of our problems than through our dreams.[1]

I hope that by now you are interested in listening to your own dreams. The problem you may be anticipating is, 'Where do I start and how do I know what my dreams are saying?' It is not the place of this book (and it really would not help anyway) to give an exhaustive list of what dream symbols can represent. The fact is that symbols often mean different things to different people at different times.

There is the famous story about the rivalry between Freud and Jung. Freud was the senior of the two and, according to the popular view of his ideas, saw the majority of dream symbols as a reference to sexual activity or organs. The two men regularly shared their dreams and endeavoured to interpret for each other. One day Jung said to Freud that he had had a dream where he was holding some eggs in his hand. 'Ah well,' said Freud, 'the symbolism of this dream is very obvious, you are undoubtedly repressing your need for sexual fulfilment.' 'But sir,' replied Jung, 'They were scrambled eggs!'

So it seems to be a safer and more balanced approach to make sure that no interpretation of dream symbols is made which does not ring true with the dreamer. It is what feels right with the individual that is the best test for arriving at a true interpretation.

Here, then, are some general guidelines for you to follow as you begin to interpret your dreams and the symbols they contain:

1. Begin by accepting that you yourself wrote the dream, and so first ask yourself, 'What am I trying to tell myself in this dream?'

2. The dream is intended to reveal and not disguise its message, so check out if it has a basic 'punch-line'. Look at the direction and nature of the feelings contained within the dream.

3. To a greater or lesser degree, the dream deals with the here and now of your life, so review recent events to see if they give clues to the dream.

4. If the dream seems to touch upon moments in the early years of your life, then examine how the effect of those days is illustrated in your life today and how this fits into the dream picture.

The next step might be to share and pray this through with a trusted friend or counsellor.

Five Types of Dream

In learning how to arrive at a right interpretation of a dream, it helps to be able to identify the *type* of dream you may be dealing with. There appear to be at least five basic types of dream that people commonly experience: the reminder dream, the warning dream, the predictive dream, the recurring dream, and the nightmare. To help you recognize these different types as they occur in your own dream life, I give below some brief examples. I also list some biblical parallels, which you may like to look up for yourself and study in more detail.

Reminder dreams

These are those dreams which pick up material which we have neglected during waking life and which we need to notice. For example, you may dream of going on holiday and finding that your passport has expired or that you have forgotten to pack something. It would be as well then, if you are about to go on holiday to check if your passport is up to date and will still be so whilst you are away. It is your way of reminding yourself that you need to make sure of some things so that you can travel with peace of mind.

Perhaps you dream of doors banging in the wind when there is no storm; it may be your way of reminding yourself that the door needs repairing and, if you do not do it, then it may be that the door will eventually come down. So just check out such items to see if you have overlooked something which in the near future could happen but which prompt action now will prevent.

Often we may dream of people we know who are in trouble or about to make a decision of importance. This is sometimes a way that God reminds us to pray and intercede for others when we have forgotten to do this. I had a reminder dream some years ago in which Jesus appeared and simply said. 'Pray for Bob, he needs your prayers.' Bob was a friend I had known from my earliest days as a Christian and we had shared a great many things together. We had both grown up in difficult family surroundings and had both been forced to move out of the family home through the divorce of our parents. Therefore we had a deep affection and interest in each other's lives. However, I had indeed not been faithful in my prayers for him and his family. So I set aside some time the following day to pray for him and for whatever needs he had. Some weeks later I was back in Birkenhead where he lived and he told me that recently he and his wife had been going through very difficult times involving a decision to give up the pastorate of a church. It had been hard to do, he said, but he had felt really supported by my prayers.

It seemed that this reminder dream had come at a very strategic time indeed. Thank God that he is faithful to remind us of our calling to pray and support one another! Consider the following examples from the Bible which are in effect reminder dreams; their importance differs according to the scale of the issue at hand.
Biblical parallels:
Genesis 15. 1–6, 12–16:   God reminds Abraham of his promises to him that he would be the father of a great nation.
1 Kings 9. 2–9:   In this second dream experience of Solomon (cf. 1 Kings 3. 5–15) God reminds him of the covenant responsibilities of the nation and the consequences of default.
cf. also Gen. 28. 11–16; Judges 7. 13–15.

Warning Dreams

These dreams operate on the same principle as the reminder dreams only they deal with material of a more personal and important nature. Many people dream of falling down stairs or of having a car crash. Whilst these dreams could be speaking in a general way about the way a person's life may be heading for a collision, it may help to check out, for example, if the stair-carpet is getting worn and whether, if not given proper attention, it might cause a falling accident. If you need to get the car in for a service and have neglected to do so, your dream may be warning you that continuing neglect could result in an accident. It could, of course, be a comment by yourself on the consequences of your present habit of driving. Above all, check out the dream with the known facts.

The warnings may relate to some issue that God has been helping

us through and reflect the consequences that may arise if we neglect
to maintain our freedom in Christ. For example, a young man who
lived in the East Midlands had received a real deliverance from a
homosexual life-style which he had been anxious to be free of.
Some months later he dreamed of standing and watching two men
engaged in love-making and felt quite aroused by all this; at other
times he would stand and watch and be repulsed by the whole affair.
He wondered if he was being attacked by the Devil and therefore
how should he tackle this whole issue. As we shared the dream
material together he remarked how difficult he found it to talk
about it all. After sharing I suggested that his dreams seemed to me
to be a warning about the consequences of standing in the place of
temptation on this issue again. His dream was telling him that he
was still open to arousal as well as being repelled by his former
homosexuality. It was a basic warning not to allow himself to be
tempted by his former associates. He smiled and said that this was
precisely what he had been allowing and that in future he would live
up to that part of the 'Lord's prayer' which says, 'Lead us not into
temptation.'

Biblical parallels

Genesis 31.24:   God spoke to Laban the Aramean concerning his
dispute with his nephew Jacob and said to him, 'Be careful not
to say anything to Jacob, either good or bad.'

Matthew 1. 20:   All these passages refer to the events surrounding
the birth of Jesus Christ. They were a mixture of warnings to
obey God and not be afraid as well as exhortations to flee from
danger. Imagine the consequences if Joseph or the wise men
had ignored these warning dreams!

Predictive Dreams

Very often we may have dreams about events which actually
happen! Ann Faraday in her book called *Dream Power*, tells of a
schoolteacher who dreamed of another teacher eloping with an
ancillary worker at the school. Some weeks later this romantic
moment took place. Others may dream of the death of a relative
which then transpires. What is most likely happening in the
majority of these examples is that the dream is playing detective. It
is making conclusions about things we may have noticed but not
paid attention to; it is putting two and two together and making
four. Should you have such a dream then do make some careful

inquiries to see if you are really paying attention to the signals of life around you. For example, the school teacher in the Faraday example did in fact remember that her colleague seemed rather happy at the time and was in the habit of whistling and singing snippets of love songs as she walked around the building. Closer recollection of events also revealed that the blue-collared worker was never around at lunch breaks when the other teacher was also absent!

However, this is not to rule out the fact that we may have a dream which opens up the future and which may concern ourselves or others whom we know. At times God may give us a dream which is to prepare us for a step of faith either on our own behalf or for another.

In 1981 I was praying about where to serve my first curacy and our family preference at that time was to remain in the East Midlands. I was asked to consider working in a parish in Bolton and our immediate response was not enthusiastic to say the least. However, we prayed as a family and decided to go and have a look at the parish. Before going up for an exploratory weekend my wife Carole had a dream of our going to the parish.

In her dream she saw the vicar and described him as a person with a cuddly, friendly face. She saw lakes and pine trees, hardly the picture either of us had of the city, especially as Carole had worked there in years gone by. The final element of the dream was that of being in a building that was too small for us and a minister, not the vicar, saying something to the effect that 'This is none other than the house of the Lord.'

Eventually we went to Bolton and Carole was quite surprised to find that Fred, the vicar, was exactly as she had seen him in the dream. On the Sunday morning we went to the parish church which was extremely spacious and had quite a large balcony. I had elected to go on to the next service which was being held by the outgoing curate in the daughter church. This was an old corrugated iron building, and a family service was being held. Jeff put up a flannel-graph illustration upon the board. He turned to the congregation and said, 'No, this is not the Town Hall, this is none other than the house of the Lord!'

You can imagine the impact that this had upon me. Before going home we decided to take a drive round the parish and think about what God was saying to us. Then, hardly realizing it, we found ourselves driving beside a huge lake studded with pine trees; it was one of four local and landscaped reservoirs. This sealed God's call for us and, although we felt no affinity for Bolton, we went in the belief that this was God's will for us. We have never regretted going, and subsequently we saw a lot of people coming to a living faith. It was one of the most thrilling experiences of our lives to date. We had been given a predictive dream to help us overcome our natural prejudices and be open to God's guidance and will for our lives. This kind of dream then is to enable a person to be prepared to take a step of faith into one of God's creative moments for us or for others.

Biblical parallels:

Genesis 37. 5–11: Part of the Joseph cycle where he dreams of future power over his brothers.

2 Sam. 7. 4–17: Nathan the prophet, following a word which came to him during his sleep, predicts that it is King David's son who will in fact build the temple in the city.

Revelation 9. 17f: Part of John's vision of the future when God will vanquish his enemies.

Note. There are, of course, dreams which are clearly predictive and, once this is apparent, the person should pray about how and with whom he or she is to share its message.

Recurring Dreams

There will be times when some dreams will recur during sleep. They may be pleasant or they may be disturbing. This is usually because such dreams deal, like nightmares, with unfinished business within our lives.

> I had such a dream for some years in my early teens which was about my being in the toilets at my primary school. I would be sitting in the cubicle and always the door would either be opened from the outside or someone would peer over the top of the door. In any case, the dream involved exposure and embarrassment.

As I later worked on these dreams I discovered that they reflected a time in my life when I was waking up to my sexuality and discovering new emotions and awarenesses. I was clearly uncomfortable for a while with this development and also had no one close to me whom I felt I could talk to seriously and objectively. The choice of dream picture was apt because I was also uncomfortable at school for some time, especially as I felt embarrassed changing clothes in front of the girls as we prepared to do physical training and the like. When I discovered the link message in the dreams the need for them ceased.

Should you be having recurring dreams then check to see if they have a 'link-message' to some other event, past or current, in your life. Once this has been discovered, it may be a good thing to share it with a trusted friend or counsellor who will pray with you through the dream.

Biblical parallels:

Genesis 41. 1–7: The Pharoah had recurring dreams about an impending famine.

Daniel 2. 1ff: A similar series of dreams for King Nebuchadnezzar, but this time about his role as a world leader.

Nightmares

We have already touched upon this kind of dream earlier in the book (pp. 29, 38–40). Suffice it to say at this point that most nightmares seem to relate to two aspects of our lives. The first concerns those fears and troublesome feelings which relate to our own impulses and instincts and with which we are still uncomfortable or unsure. The other is that of objective experiences from earlier encounters, often childhood traumas.

Biblical parallels:

Job 7. 14; 33. 14–18: The dreamer knows that he has unfinished business concerning his walk with God and so nightmares become the vehicle for God to press home his word.

Daniel 4. 5ff: The King states that the images and visions of his dreams terrify him.

Matthew 27. 19: Pilate's wife has obviously been considering what has been happening to Jesus and she is troubled in heart and mind.

Four Dimensions of Dreaming

Having looked at some examples of the different types of dream that are commonly experienced, we can now go on to explore the four dimensions in which dreams can occur. Whatever the type of dream you may be trying to interpret, it is crucial that you determine the dimension of your life to which the dream relates. Does it relate to the people, objects and events which influence your life from the world outside? Or does it relate to your own inner world of consciousness, the world of your personal thoughts and emotions? Could the dream be a message from the deeper, unconscious dimension of your mind? Or could it even be a dream that is operating in a spiritual dimension – a dream from God?

The influence of the outside world

The first dimension of dreaming relates to the constant influence of the outside world on the general course of our everyday lives. Much of this influence is received at 'gut' level, and we may not always give it sufficient notice during waking life. If, then, we find we are dreaming about people, objects or events with which we are familiar, it is as well to ask ourselves whether the dream is saying something objectively about these things themselves, or whether the dream is using these things as symbols which relate to some other dimension of our existence. For example, when we dream of friends or family we need to work out whether the dream refers directly to them (i.e. does it tally with our experience of them?) or whether they represent something else.

A dream, then, can reveal how we really view the world around us. Call it subjective reality – we could be mistaken in our view – nonetheless the dream shows what we really feel or think. It is as well therefore to check out as many of the facts of a situation before we act prematurely in response to our dream. Riffel offers some good advice here. He suggests that the first thing to do when we feel we have an interpretation is to go directly to God in prayer for confirmation. Then check it out with Scripture (since God does not contradict himself in his guidance and truth) and seek confirmation from friends who won't just agree with you for politeness sake. I would also advise you to listen to the feelings that come out of the dream and see how these match up with how you have previously felt about whatever the dream contains.

The inner world of the dreamer

If our dreams do not appear to be offering any objective insights, then it could be that we need to move on to a second level of approach. The dream may be operating in the dimension of your own inner world of thoughts and emotions. Faraday speaks of the dream as having a 'through the looking glass' dimension, causing it to act rather like a distorting mirror.[2] In this kind of dreaming we may incorporate actual or imaginary people in our lives as symbols to represent feelings or ideas which we are trying to express.

For example, someone may dream of the Queen Mother coming for tea. For most of us the Queen Mother would not be someone we have a relationship with, but she might represent for us royalty, or someone important. And so having this special mother enter your dreams may be your way of saying 'As far as I am concerned, I have someone who is important to me coming to tea, or meet with me,' etc. The next step would be to examine the feelings and circumstances of the dream in the light of this important encounter. We also need a word of caution here about dreaming of friends and family. The meaning of such dreams depends usually upon what the characters are doing, what is our response to them and the general circumstance of the dream. Again, the question to be asked is, 'What does the dream tell me about my present feelings and thoughts regarding this person?'

We may dream of our parents who may well represent themselves or be our way of talking about authority figures who may be inhibiting our progress in life. There are of course other authority figures we may dream of, such as policemen, doctors and nurses and school-teachers.

> I had a dream recently in which I was driving a car with Carole, my wife, as passenger, when suddenly a police car seemed to pounce upon us from behind and caused us to stop the car. I knew that I had committed no crime and so wondered what the policeman wanted with us. The police officer began to upbraid my wife and say that she would never drive again. I felt very angry but powerless to help.

When I awoke I thought about the dream and also remembered that the police officer also said that there would be no more blessing as a result of what my wife had done. I immediately recognized that the dream reflected my wife's situation and present dilemma. Though a licensed deaconness in the Church of England, she has not as yet been given a parish to work in. We have also been told that our bishop will not allow us to serve together in the same parish at any time. In our attempts to resolve the situation we have been trying to persuade our bishop to open a door of ministry for Carole, although we have often wondered if we have been making things more difficult for ourselves by doing so. The police officer in the dream obviously represented ecclesiastical authority against which we have been feeling powerless. The clue to the ecclesiastical connection hinged on the reference to blessing in the dream.

We may dream of friends or acquaintances whom we have not seen for many years and, if so, it is more than likely that we are utilizing this person to think about some more present-day event. It could be that their personality, circumstance or even name 'has something to say to us'. Some years ago I had a dream of being in two theological colleges which I had actually attended but with a gap of some twelve years in between. At both places I was meeting a teacher, called Felicity Lawson, who taught at the second college in my dream. In real life I know Felicity as a friend as well. So as I examined the dream I began to see that it was not an objective comment about Felicity but that her name represented an issue I had been working on. It was at a time when I was gathering material for a thesis on the subject of dreams. I was becoming more and more convinced that our dreams function according to a number of principles, one of which is that we are wholly truthful to ourselves when we sleep. To gather material I had written to a number of students from a range of theological colleges asking for volunteers to record dreams and then send them to me. The name, Felicity Lawson, spoke directly to my research; there was a law or principle of truth, of appropriateness (felicity) at work within our dreams. I found this dream message very reassuring and it encouraged me to continue with my research into dreams.

When we dream about animals they are more than likely to represent some quality we find in ourselves or those whom they represent. The ferocious beasts of Nebuchadnezzar's dreams easily spoke of the war-like attitude of his contemporary super-powers. Sometimes we may dream of being chased by animals. Riffel recommends that if this is the case that we extend the dream picture, stop running and face the on-rushing animal. The result may indicate whether the animal represents you or somebody else.[3] Should the animal become friendly, then it could be a dream picture about our own temperament that has gone wild and needs to come back under our control. Animals could also be a reference to our basic instincts such as our sexuality or even our eating habits. They can be useful symbols of those whom we know. Peter the Apostle, you remember, had his roof-top vision of animals of an uneatable kind. It was a prophetic vision referring to Peter's own reluctance to share the good news with Gentile races which his Judaism pronounced unclean.

Our dreams teem with symbols. From animals to houses; from friends to familiar themes such as flying or losing one's teeth. Some seem to speak loud and clear of their own accord, others need to be deciphered along the lines already suggested. The way into the symbol is to ask how we are feeling about it. We may need to ask, 'Who or what does this remind me of?' Another approach would be to use the *gestalt* method already demonstrated in chapter 6.

Dreams from the unconscious

The third dimension of dream content reflects the unconscious attitudes, conflicts and fears of the dreamer. These dreams offer a picture of the individual's deeper self. It is the kind of dream which tells us why we have acquired certain behaviour patterns in life. Here the symbols are more likely to represent the parts of ourselves which we may have had difficulty in accepting as our own. Jung would call this the 'shadow' part of our lives. For example, a Christian friend and minister had a recurring dream of walking along a road and meeting a very attractive woman for whom he felt strong desires of affection. As he was happily married and wanted very much to be faithful to his Lord, he was quite concerned about whether he was being led astray with sexual fantasies. I suggested to him that the female could well be speaking of the more creative and sensitive side of his nature which he had more or less repressed in his life. He was a gifted communicator but had found it hard to let people see this other facet of his abilities. He immediately recognized himself in the symbol of the woman. Later he wrote that this discovery had given some release and benefit to his life. He was beginning to get in touch with his 'shadow self', and one of the ways in which this was facilitated was to relive the dream picture and then to say to the woman, 'I know who you are and I welcome you and invite you to share your life and talent with me.'

Very often this kind of dream may bring to the surface some of the conflicts we have been unwilling to face in waking life. We can allow the dream to speak for itself and, when appropriate, use the *gestalt* method, to clarify the nature of the conflict. Compare the following dream account which a married woman shared:

> I have been told that my daughter is dead and so I went home to see her body. When I got there I was told she was in a coffin upstairs. I was invited to go and see her but I just couldn't bring myself to do it. So I stayed downstairs and tried to get on with other things.

I suggested that we re-ran the dream picture and saw where she could take the dream story. She then went on to describe how eventually she went upstairs and looked inside the coffin itself. There was a certain amount of reluctance about this, but to her surprise she discovered that there was no body inside. Then she said that she felt that somehow it was she herself whom she had feared to be dead and not her daughter. Continuing the dream picture she said that she came back downstairs and went into her study where her mother was tidying up her papers. 'She's always doing things like that,' she said. It became obvious here that there had been a long-standing conflict of wills between her and her mother. It was at this point then that it was decided she would act out a needed confrontation with her mother over how she wanted her study things left alone. She began to tell her mother softly to leave her things alone. Playing the part of her mother, I resisted her wishes in much the same vein as her mother did according to the dream picture. Very quickly the woman began to cry and break down a little at the opposition and chiding of her 'mother'. Gone was the calm that was on the surface, and into the forefront came the repressed anger at not being able to live as she wanted to. The counselling which followed revealed that this good lady, a professional helper in her own right, had always found it difficult to confront her mother and live according to her own interests and outlook. The dead daughter in the dream was her independent and creative self which she feared might die through this continuous friction. As a result of this dream work she was able to own her own freer self and be more determined to allow this side of her life more expression in future. There was also the determination to forgive her mother and, in the name of Jesus, to be forgiven for holding any bitter feelings towards her.

Dreams from God

Finally, in this section on dream dimensions, let me say a little about the spiritual dream. By this I mean a dream which is a word from God to us. When we regard the dream experience with respect, God is able to share his word of guidance and challenge with us. Dr T. J. Barnardo maintained that his life's work among the destitute poor was the result of dreams he was having at a time of uncertainty in his mind. His dreams provided him with the right guidance to give up ideas of working with the China Inland Mission and to concentrate on needs he had found in the streets of London.[5] We have already mentioned the dreams of Paul by which his missionary work was redirected into Macedonia, and so opening the gateway for the gospel to come to Europe.

These spiritual dreams can address a host of subjects, and they can be quite direct. Consider, for example, the simple and direct nature of the warning dreams in the Nativity accounts. God's word to Solomon, as he lay sleeping on the eve of the consecration of the new temple, is both direct and far-reaching; through it Solomon chose to be a wise leader of his people.

What is noticeable about this category of dream is that the symbolic element is largely replaced by a simple dialogue between God and man. Even Peter's roof-top experience of the ceremonially unclean animals gains authority only when God says, 'Do not call unclean what I have called clean.' This is not to say that God cannot impinge upon our own dreams with indications of his word or will for us; after all this corresponds with how God works in our waking lives anyway. These dreams, like any other, are to be carefully considered and shared and then prayerfully acted upon. What is more, we should expect God to give dreams of this kind. Peter's word on the day of Pentecost implied, amongst other things, that the spiritual outpouring would include continual dreaming. We have seen that our own dreams tap into our capacity to be really sensitive to our inner lives and spirit; how much more then should the Holy Spirit make us sensitive to God's word as we dream and enjoy his gift of sleep!

Recording your Dreams

Most people do not remember their dreams because they do not consider them important enough. I hope that, by the time you have reached this part of the book, you have more interest in your dream life. Attitudes like 'Why bother?' or 'Dreams are just silly, aren't they?' and 'They're not worth paying attention to,' effectively cut our dreams from our memory. So the first step we need to take in recording our dreams is to respect them and say we want to hear and learn from them. Here is a simple prayer you can use to help open the door to your dream recall:

> Heavenly Father, I thank you that you grant to those you love the blessing of sleep. Please help me to accept myself completely and to rejoice in the knowledge that you love me completely. I ask you now to help me remember my dreams. I really want to know myself better so

that I can love you more, through Jesus Christ my Lord. Amen.

This deals with the spiritual preparation but there are also some
practical steps which we can take. You may believe that you are one
of those people who does not dream. Now it is a known fact that
the average dreamer goes through the cycle of dreaming about four
or five times a night (see chapter 3). So a simple way to pinpoint a
dream is to set your alarm clock for approximately two hours after
you have gone to bed (a time likely to be a REM period), and then
on for periods of about 2 hours. This should enable you to awake
with a dream in your mind. Should the idea of continual awakening
not appeal to you, you can set your alarm for a time of one to one and
a half hours before you normally awake. Then follow through the
practical suggestions listed below.

Keeping a dream diary

1. Always keep pen and paper beside your bed.
2. Make sure you have access to a light; it is better not to use too
   bright a light as too sharp an awakening can disturb dream
   recall.

Note: Too loud an alarm can have the same effect.

3. Before going to sleep prepare yourself with a prayer where you
   say aloud that you want to hear from your dreams.
4. When you awake, immediately write down as much dream
   detail as you can. Resist the temptation to go back to sleep!
5. Add as many associations to your dream as you can, including
   links into recent events which seem to fit the dream story. Add
   any feelings either contained in your dream or which arise as a
   result of the dream.
6. What does the dream appear to be saying at first glance?
7. Write the dream down whilst you are still in bed; do not try to
   carry it around as you prepare yourself for the rest of the day.

Note: Do not forget to date your dreams as this is often helpful later
when you are working with your dream and you want to associate it
with events at that time.

8. Now commit your dreams and any thoughts they have brought
   to God in prayer. In this way your morning prayers will include what you have been reviewing during sleep. Any truths,
   challenges and convictions must be likewise committed to
   the Lord, with the resolve to take whatever action seems
   appropriate.

9. If you find it difficult to understand your dreams then try the *gestalt* approach; give each part of your dream a voice and see if this takes you further into knowing about your dream. It often helps to share your dreams and thoughts with a trusted friend who knows and appreciates you to some degree.

Conclusion

Dreams are part of the everyday (or night) experience of all peoples. There is not space in this book to mention the way in which other cultures and religions use dreams.[6] They form part of the normal process by which we function and develop as individuals. Scientific research, as well as the experience of working with dreams, convince us that 'dreaming is good for you'. To ignore dreams is to shut out what we really think about a third of our lives. To regard dreams as only the result of an over-active digestive system is to be in danger of blocking out the emotional and spiritual insights that they can bring to our lives. Not to welcome them as part of our real selves is both to deny who we are as well as to close our hearts to one way in which God may share his prophetic word for our lives.

Further, to work with our dreams is to learn more about who we are and what we are feeling about people and things at every level of our lives. This I have discovered is a road to healing, if we share all this with the God who loves us and made us so in the first place.

'Let us then all, deliver ourselves to the interpretation of dreams; men, women, young and old, rich and poor ... sleep offers itself to all.'[7]

Notes

1 I have a dream

1. *Sunday Express*, 1 March 1981.

2 The Bible and dreams

1. Herman Riffel,*Your Dreams: God's Neglected Gift* (Kingsway Publications, 1984),p. 22.
2. Visions of the night: Gen. 46. 2. Job 20. 18; 33. 15. Isa. 29. 7. Dan. 2. 9; 7. 7,13. Acts 16. 9; 18. 9.   Visions of the head: Dan. 2. 28; 4. 5, 10, 13.
3. Heaven: Num. 24. 4. Ezek. 1 1; 40. 2. 2 Cor. 12. 1–4.   Spiritual battles: 1 Sam. 3. 15. Dan. 9. 21–4.   Prophetic challenges: Isa. 1. 1; 22. 5. Ezek. 7. 13; 11. 24. Nahum 1. 1.   End times: Isa. 21. 2. Dan. 8. 17. Mic. 3. 6. Rev. 9. 17.
4. Arthur Janov, *The Primal Scream*, (Abacus Books, 1976), pp. 264–5.
5. cf. Gen. 41. 16; 'I cannot do it,' Joseph replied to Pharoah, 'But God will give Pharoah the answer he desires.'
6. cf. Deut. 13. 1–5.

3 Twentieth-century dreaming

1 See R. Parker, *Dreams and Spirituality* (Grove Books, 1985), pp. 17–18. A fuller description of the historic interest in dreams since the times of the early Church can be found in chapter 1 ('Evolution in dreaming') of my 'Dreams as a Religious Phenomenon' (unpublished M. Th. thesis at Nottingham University), pp. 9–22.
2. See the notes on Ian Oswald's findings regarding brain-cell renewal and REM sleep on p. 19 of *Dreams and Spirituality*.
3. Ann Faraday, *Dream Power* (Pan Books, 1972), pp. 11–12.
4. Sigmund Freud, *The Interpretation of Dreams* (Penguin Books, 1975), p. 199.

5. Ibid., page 305.
6. Carl Jung, *Modern Man in Search of A Soul* (Routledge, 1933), p. 5.
7. Ibid., p. 264.
8. Faraday, *Dream Power* p. 112.
9. C. S. Hall, *The Meaning of Dreams* (New York, McGraw Hill, 1953, 1966).
10. For a fuller treatment of this outline, compare it with the four-fold process outlined by Roger Hurding in *Roots and Shoots*, (Hodder and Stoughton, 1985), p. 204.
11. Ann Faraday, *The Dream Game*, (Penguin Books, 1976), p. 130.

4 Opening the dream door

1. *Dreams and Spirituality*, Grove Books (Spirituality Series, no. 15).
2. cf. Mark 4. 10–13, 33–4.
3. cf. also Judg. 7. 13; Dan. 5. 12.
4. D. Hunt and T. A. McMahon, *The Seduction of Christianity*. Christian Life Publishers, 1985.

5 Praying with dreams

1. cf. Rev. 1. 17; 5. 4; 19. 10; 21. 8.
2. cf. Gen. 28. 11–22; 1 Kings 3. 5–15.
3. *Didache* 11. 4 ff.
4. Tertullian, 'On the Soul', in A. C. Coxe (ed.), *Ante-Nicene Fathers*, vol. 3 (T. & T. Clark, 1980), pp. 37, 343, 558, 609f, 699.
5. Gregory of Nyssa, 'On the Making of Man', in P. Schaff and H. Wace (eds), *Nicene and Post-Nicene Fathers*, second series, vol. 5 (T. & T. Clark, 1980), p. 142.
6. Parker, *Dreams and Spirituality*, p. 22.

6 Healing with dreams

1. A verbatim account of a shared counselling session at St John's College, Nottingham, in July 1986 (used with permission).
2. Janov, *The Primal Scream*, p. 262f.
3. See the general ban on all things occultic in Deuteronomy 18. 9–13.

7 Dreams for the people
1. Bill Subritzky, *Demons Defeated* (Sovereign World, 1985), pp. 15–19.
2. K. McAll, *Healing the Family Tree* (Sheldon Press, 1982), pp. 44–5.

8 Getting on with dreams
1. Riffel, *Your Dreams*, p. 14.
2. Faraday, *Dream Power*, p. 142.
3. Riffel, *Your Dreams*, p. 51.
4. Incidentally, the acting out of dreams using role-play is not that much different to the 'acted parable' used by some of the prophets to communicate the message of their vision. Consider for example Isaiah, who walked naked through the streets of Jerusalem to indicate the fate of the conquered nation about to be exiled. Ezekiel made a mock-up of the city of Jerusalem being besieged as a comment upon what was happening to an unfaithful nation. Then there is Agabus's prophetic way of tying Paul with a leather belt in order to illustrate the imprisonment that awaited Paul if he went to Jerusalem. All three of these men had seen in their vision what they later enacted.
5. Gillian Wagner, *Barnardo*, (Eyre and Spottiswode, 1980), pp. 10, 79.
6. See my thesis 'Dreams as a Religious Phenomenon', 1980.
7. Synesius of Cyrene, 4th-century Church writer.